Taxi Driver

Paul Schrader is a noted critic, screenwriter and director. By his mid-twenties he had already been a film reviewer for the *LA Free Press*, while a graduate student at UCLA; editor of his own magazine, *Cinema*; Fellow in Criticism of the American Film Institute; and author of the uncompromising *Transcendental Style in Film: Ozu, Bresson, Dreyer*. By the mid-seventies he was one of Hollywood's most successful screenwriters, eventually writing three films for Martin Scorsese: *Taxi Driver*, *Raging Bull*, and *The Last Temptation of Christ*. His directorial achievements include *Blue Collar*, *American Gigolo*, *Mishima*, *Patty Hearst*, *The Comfort of Strangers*, and *Light Sleeper*.

by the same author

LIGHT SLEEPER
SCHRADER ON SCHRADER
edited by Kevin Jackson

Taxi Driver

Paul Schrader

faber and faber

First published in 1990
by Faber and Faber Limited
3 Queen Square London WC1N 3AU

Published in the United States by Faber and Faber Inc.
a division of Farrar, Straus and Giroux Inc.
New York

Typeset by Wilmaset Ltd, Birkenhead, Wirral
Printed in England by Clays Ltd, St Ives plc

Paul Schrader is hereby identified as author
of this work in accordance with Section 77 of
the Copyright, Designs and Patents Act 1988

Stills courtesy of BFI Stills, Posters and Design

A CIP record for this book is available from the British Library

ISBN 0–571–14464–0

13 15 17 19 20 18 16 14 12

Contents

Paul Schrader, Martin Scorsese
and Robert De Niro during the
making of *Taxi Driver*

Introduction

This interview was conducted for Cahiers du Cinéma *on 29 January 1982 at Martin Scorsese's apartment in lower Manhattan. Marty had spent the night editing* The King of Comedy; *I had spent the night researching after-hours clubs on the upper West Side. As 7 a.m. light streamed through the Hudson River windows, we began our conversation. During the first hour we discussed American movies; the second, our collaborations.*

1

PAUL SCHRADER: What movies were you attracted to as an
   adolescent?

MARTIN SCORSESE: There are many, many films – I'll just talk
   about what first comes to mind. The first image I remember
   seeing in a movie theatre – my father used to take me
   because of my asthma – was a trailer in Trucolor of Roy
   Rogers and his horse jumping over a log. My father said,
   'Do you know what Trigger is?' I said, 'That's trigger.'
   (Scorsese pulls the trigger of an imaginary gun.) I was about
   three or four years old. My father said, 'No, that's the name
   of the horse.' And there was this beautiful horse and this
   guy with fringe jumping and flying in the air like an angel.
   Ever since I always wanted to be a cowboy and never was.

SCHRADER: Between the ages of seven and ten, what movies
   would you prefer?

SCORSESE: Mainly westerns. *Duel in the Sun.* My mother took me
   to see it even though it was condemned from the pulpit. My
   father didn't go. For some strange reason the film was very
   effective on me. To this day I love the picture. And somehow
   I couldn't watch the ending; I had to cover my eyes. It seemed
   like a horror story. The two lovers loved each other so much
   they had to kill each other. Even to this day.

SCHRADER: At what point did puberty set into your movie-
   going experience? Who were the first women, as women,
   that you saw on the screen and sexually desired?

SCORSESE: Wanted them, or was interested in what they looked like?

SCHRADER: Both.

SCORSESE: And what they felt like when you touched them?

SCHRADER: Yeah.

SCORSESE: Bypassing Barbara Britton – I was in love with her. Crazy. You see, Barbara Britton and John Paine were my favourites.

SCHRADER: How old were you at that time?

SCORSESE: About ten. *I shot Jesse James*. Barbara Britton's in it, you know. I remember being on a bus, being taken to see it. I remember thinking, what's the matter with these people? Don't they realize *I Shot Jesse James* is playing? They're on a bus, what's the matter with them? Why aren't they going to the theatre?

SCHRADER: She was your first screen crush?

SCORSESE: Then in '56, Elizabeth Taylor on the cover of *Life* magazine in a still from *Giant*, sitting on a bed. She was very beautiful. Oh, however, there's Jean Simmons in *Great Expectations*. That was a killer. Always been a killer.

SCHRADER: As you know, I wasn't allowed to go to movies as a child. One of the first films I saw was *Wild in the Country* with Presley and Tuesday Weld. Tuesday was sixteen at the time and was my first major movie crush. One of my strangest experiences when I came to Hollywood was sitting in a screening room next to Tuesday Weld. I thought she lived on another planet.

SCORSESE: I'm trying to think. Women never really interested me that much in movies. I wonder why that is . . .

SCHRADER: I have to take exception, because having just read *Jerusalem, Jerusalem* (*Scorsese's first script, preceding* Who's that Knocking at my Door?), I'm aware of the enormous sexual impact of the movies on you.

SCORSESE: One of the first sexual images I remember from film, besides *Duel in the Sun*, which I couldn't look at for some reason unknown to me, was *Peter Pan*. In one scene where Wendy had to cross over a rock and she lifts her dress and you see her calf and that's absolutely wonderful. Disney had everything. Michael Powell is right, Disney was a true genius. She had a wonderful leg. I'm serious. It was really a shock. I said, 'This is it. I'm in love with Wendy.'

SCHRADER: Old Walt knew where the buttons were . . .

SCORSESE: I think the first time we met I told you this. My aunt, Aunt Mary, who was a very tough lady, took me to see a double bill of *Bambi* and *Out of the Past* . . .

SCHRADER: Of Mitchum, Douglas or Greer, which one did you identify with?

SCORSESE: Forget the women, I just remember the raincoats. But all during the film I kept asking, 'When is *Bambi* coming on?' My aunt kept saying, 'Shut up, this is good, I'll kill you.'

SCHRADER: By twelve, you were starting to get the itch between your legs.

SCORSESE: That of course was like *High School Confidential* with Jerry Lee Lewis and *Blackboard Jungle*. Sex came on the screen with the music and you knew it. My father was sitting next to me and he was shocked. When the MGM logo came on and you heard Bill Haley – I mean the film was not the best, but it was for me . . .

SCHRADER: Strictly below the waist.

SCORSESE: Right.

SCHRADER: At what point did your love of neighbourhood movies merge with an awareness of foreign films?

SCORSESE: My father bought a 16-inch TV set in 1948. At that time they showed a lot of features on TV. Every other Friday night they would show Italian films . . .

SCHRADER: Subtitled?

SCORSESE: Absolutely. They showed *Paisa* and *Bicycle Thieves*, and my grandmother would cry, and my mother would cry. They didn't want to see it 'cause the men were in the war, but the men wanted to. The women got very upset.

SCHRADER: There wasn't any clear demarcation between American and foreign films? They merged together?

SCORSESE: Yes, except that we made the Westerns.

SCHRADER: Was there a point when American movies diverged from non-American movies?

SCORSESE: 1958, when I discovered Bergman for myself. When I was in high school and not doing well at preparatory seminary all the Bergman films had titles like *Monika* and *A*

Secret Shame of Love. All on the Condemned List. *Smiles of a Summer Night* I went to see and to this day I still don't understand . . .

SCHRADER: Yes, somewhere in my adolescent imagination *Smiles of a Summer Night* and *The Immoral Mr T's* were equated . . .

SCORSESE: I finally saw *The Immoral Mr T's* when I was twenty-two. I never had the guts to go to those theatres. At the same time, however, I saw *Seventh Seal* and I realized that, of course, all the great film-makers were in Europe. For about three years I had that sense of snobbism that American films were bad. Then in 1961 I read, in *Film Culture*, Andrew Sarris's article based on the theories of *Cahiers*, the *politique des auteurs*, which is old history now. But I went through the lists and underlined every one of the films I saw and put a star next to the ones I liked. Of all the directors, I found I liked the 'pantheon' directors most. I liked John Ford's films best – and they weren't all Westerns either.

SCHRADER: At this point you realized you could express ideas through films –

SCORSESE: But *Seventh Seal* is highly emotional as well. When the penitents come in – that speech is extraordinary.

SCHRADER: I noticed you quoted *Diary of a Country Priest* in *Jerusalem, Jerusalem*. When did you see it?

SCORSESE: Around 1964. I must make a confession. It's very difficult for me to watch it again. That and *Ordet*.

SCHRADER: I see them once a year. *Voyage in Italy* is difficult for me . . .

SCORSESE: *Voyage in Italy* I can watch over and over again. I cry and get crazy. But those two pictures and *Europa 51* – it's amazing. I really can't take it any more. I can't do it. I can't handle it.

SCHRADER: Let me ask you another question. (*Consults some scribbled notes.*) Let's see, I wrote this down a couple of hours ago when I was about as awake as I am now. Do you want history to remember you?

SCORSESE: I can be glib and say let's both be pretentious, right? I'm not sure I would answer that if someone else asked me.

But again, my ego is enormous. I love that problem. Yes, most likely I would. I don't know why.

SCHRADER: If you had to choose . . .

SCORSESE: The thing about being remembered is that it replaces fate and the salvation of the soul. How could you replace that? You can't.

SCHRADER: If you had to choose between being remembered or fulfilled, which would you choose?

SCORSESE: It would have to be fulfilled. You have to be content with yourself. Not necessarily happy, you could be miserable but fulfilled.

SCHRADER: So fuck history when it comes to personal fulfilment?

SCORSESE: It's a hard thing to replace what you really believe in. The salvation of the soul, whether it's Presbyterian, Jewish, Catholic or whatever. You know what I'm saying? If you don't have any belief in it now, you're dead.

SCHRADER: When I was in Amsterdam last year – I think we talked about this before – I was giving a lecture and I went to the Rijksmuseum, probably the best organized museum in the world. All devoted to Van Gogh, totally devoted and organized around thirty-nine miserable, increasingly tormented years of a man's life. And I remember in the middle of the lecture I was overwhelmed by an awareness: I said to the audience, 'If someone came to me right now and offered me a deal – if he said, we'll build you a museum if you will live a life like Van Gogh's' – and I said –

SCORSESE: I think I have to pass.

SCHRADER: Exactly.

SCORSESE: That drive has been replaced.

SCHRADER: Was there a point when it was more important to be remembered?

SCORSESE: Yeah, when I was trying to get *Mean Streets* made. When I tried experiments in *Alice* and *Taxi Driver*. I never thought *Taxi* would make a dime. I just came across some 8 mm footage of you and me and Vernon Zimmerman bowling in LA. It's wonderful. It just came out of storage. I put it all together.

SCHRADER: I don't remember.

SCORSESE: It's wonderful. It's beautiful because it's just about a month before it happened. With Michael and Julia (*Phillips, the producers of* Taxi Driver) that Sunday morning after it opened and it was successful. We made that film because we felt something – the *Notes from the Underground* thing.

SCHRADER: That's a blessing of success. It allows you to live without worrying about being remembered.

SCORSESE: You know, when we made *Taxi* that was like a major, major footnote for my life. Because that was it. If somebody a thousand years from now finds that thing and there's no credits on it – and if there were credits on it but they couldn't read them – but they understood what it was. Even then, it's not being remembered . . .

SCHRADER: To a god unknown . . .

SCORSESE: Exactly. The process of making the film for me was more important than the final result. And you know the second week I threatened to stop. I loved it so much I wanted to kill it. If it was not going to be done the right way, kill it. If someone is going to take it away it might as well be you. It's your duty to kill it. It's almost like the end of a movie I've seen many times, *The Horse's Mouth*, where Alec Guinness destroys the wall. He figures, 'I might as well do it.' Fuck it. His performance carries the whole thing. It's wonderful. In any event, I was doing a balancing act at that time. *Mean Streets*. I never thought it would be released, you know. I said, at least if somebody picks up this movie twenty years from now they'll see what Italian-Americans look and talk like. I was very surprised when people picked up on it.

SCHRADER: But you had ambitions, hopes you can't deny . . .

SCORSESE: Right, but I had already made a picture for Roger Corman. So, *Mean Streets* goes on the shelf, I make another picture for Roger. But at least I made an Italian-American movie that supposedly nobody wanted to see.

SCHRADER: I just won't let you get away with saying you had no aspirations for that movie.

SCORSESE: No, no. It was my whole life. The only other thing that gave me that fire was *Taxi*.

SCHRADER: Do you consider yourself 100 per cent American?

SCORSESE: Yeah.

SCHRADER: If you no longer work in this country, where would you work?

SCORSESE: You're assuming I would even continue to make pictures. That's something we talked about before. Then, it would seem to me, I'd have one major drawback, my ear for language. I think I have a certain thing for dialogue, words and phrases, and I think I would be very hurt if I didn't know a language inside and out.

SCHRADER: Would you like to work in Italy?

SCORSESE: I would try. I have a problem with the Italian language. I'm serious. I know French better than Italian. I never went to Rome until 1970. Now, with my wife, we travel back and forth. But even though I know French better I'm still not comfortable with it. My ear for Italian is very good: the gestures, moves, guttural sounds – I don't care what the words are. However, I have a problem learning Italian because my grandparents were very severe and they would take care of my brother and I during the day. They would yell at me, 'You're younger and your brother speaks better Italian.' It's the older brother syndrome. *Raging Bull* comes out of that. So I have a block against Italian. I've taken it in school, I lived in Italy; I speak it somewhat, but very badly.

SCHRADER: What American films or scenes have stayed with you longest: have affected your life emotionally, philosophically, sexually . . .?

SCORSESE: Are you going to give me a second or two?

SCHRADER: Yeah.

SCORSESE: I've got a long list.

SCHRADER: So do I.

SCORSESE: Obviously, *Public Enemy*, which still holds up. The use of music is extraordinary. At the end it's all source music. No scoring. At the end when the body falls they're playing 'I'm Forever Blowing Bubbles'. When I was thirteen years old in 1956, after I graduated from grammar school, me and Joe Morales and another guy went to see *The Searchers* at the Criterion Theatre. Walked in in the middle. And I've lived with that picture over the years. *The Red Shoes*. Renoir's *The River*. The way he used music. He goes into a sequence where they talk about Krishna and suddenly it becomes a musical.

SCHRADER: The things which come back to me are more isolated and I think fewer. Jimmy Stewart crying next to his horse in *Naked Spur*, John Wayne not allowing Jeffrey Hunter to look in *The Searchers*, when Kim Novak walks into the green neon-lit room in *Vertigo*, Quinlan investigating the Mexican boy in *Touch of Evil*, the water scene in *Sunrise*. You seem to be talking more in technical terms . . .

SCORSESE: No, no. I'm not talking technical. I'm talking about having a great time. For the last ten years I can look at *Touch of Evil* and have a ball. When I first saw it, I was dissecting it. I remember the emotion of a French film by Allegret with Gérard Philippe, in English called *The Proud and the Beautiful*, in French *Les Orgueilleux*. *That's* one of the great sexy scenes of all time. Michelle Morgan alone in the room with the fan and the half-slip and the bra – forget it. You want to see that scene? I'm glad this is a French publication because maybe somebody can help me. I've tried everybody. Nobody can get the print for me. You want to rent it in America, they send you the 16 mm print, terrific, etc. – except that scene is missing. And it's about a six-minute scene. You can't get a complete 35 of it, you can't get a 16 – it's impossible. The sexuality of that, when I was fifteen years old, was very important.

SCHRADER: Hopefully this interview will put the Cinémathèque on the trail.

SCORSESE: I'm talking about an emotional level. You talk about green rooms, but when I saw *Vertigo* I was scared. I don't know why. I loved that I was scared, I loved the picture.

SCHRADER: For me it's the most sexual of American films.

SCORSESE: I couldn't think of it in those terms at all. It was a mystery, not a whodunnit, but a sense of doom and fate. When the man comes up in the last shot we're all dead. We're all going to hell and that's it.

2

SCHRADER: I'd like to ask you some personal questions. After all, the blood is already on the sheet. You and De Niro and I have collaborated on two films and now possibly a third. How do you view this relationship?

SCORSESE: Right now?

SCHRADER: At a working stage.

SCORSESE: How do I work with De Niro? Is that what you're asking?

SCHRADER: Yes, and me.

SCORSESE: It's very interesting. I worked with Harvey Keitel on *Who's That Knocking?* Later I met Bob through Brian De Palma, and I knew Bob in a different way. I loved what he did in *Mean Streets*, and it was an absolutely collaborative effort. But somehow during that period, Bob found – although, as you know, Bob can be very quiet whereas Harvey and I talk and talk and talk – Bob found he was interested in certain things, the things you are interested in, the same way. And one of them was *Taxi Driver*. And we all felt the same way about that, OK, it was a labour of love. But the point is this: *New York, New York* became a testing ground for me and Bob. We could play around, doing improvisations, not knowing if we would ever work together again. It was a very difficult shooting period. Twenty-two weeks. When you shoot that long, you try to do something of your own, your personal life starts to fall apart – the old story, as you know. Particularly in this film with artificial sets and improvisational techniques. In any event that was a strong testing ground for me and Bob. Somehow we shipped it together. In other words, we had the same comings together and partings. We wanted to say the same things in different ways. In *Raging Bull*, for example, he never said what he wanted to say, I never said what I wanted to say, but it's all there. We are both satisfied. I'm not satisfied with whether it's a good or bad film but that we got out what we wanted to say. Then you came in at that point. You want me to talk about that too?

SCHRADER: First I'll tell you how I view my role. There's seven or eight directors I would like to work for.

SCORSESE: That's a lot.

SCHRADER: Unfortunately most of those seven or eight directors do not respect my freedom as a writer because they want to write themselves. Somebody has to play the pipe and somebody has to do the jig and I'm a bad dancer. You are one of the few, if not the only, director I've worked with that respects me as a writer. On the other hand, I'm smart enough to respect you as a director. I feel I deliver three things: theme, character, structure. Bam, bam, bam. That's my job. I give you that then I walk away.

SCORSESE: Yeah, but you're also writing dialogue. Lines like 'Suck on this' (*from* Taxi Driver), which I take seriously . . .

SCHRADER: I've found – maybe I'm paranoid – that most directors have a hard time accepting the writer's theme, character, structure.

SCORSESE: In the case of *Raging Bull*, we asked you to come in. I've always hated this discussion because Mardik Martin (*the author of the first* Raging Bull *script*) is like a brother to me. New Year's Eve I realized we've known each other for twenty years. The person I've been closest to for twenty years. He has been with me through all my crises, all the good times, all the bad times. We started writing the script of *Raging Bull* during *New York, New York*. I just want to say for the record, the poor guy, I never gave him any direction. I was running around writing the script of *New York, New York* – what we would shoot the next morning. Everybody was working on it, Earl (*MacRauch, the screenwriter*), Irwin (*Winkler, the producer*), Julia, my second wife. I didn't want that to happen again, but when Mardik came in with *Raging Bull* it was like *Rashomon*. He got twenty-five versions of the story because all the characters were alive. Bob and I felt that if you came in for six weeks, no matter what the price, it was important. And I still hadn't made up my mind about directing the picture, by the way. When we met at Musso-Frank's, you came up with one image right away – that of masturbating in the cell, which was never in the film, which is OK because it's in there anyway . . .

SCHRADER: I still think it's one of the best scenes I ever wrote.

(I'm referring to a three-page masturbation soliloquy by Jake LaMotta in solitary confinement.)

SCORSESE: On paper it was beautiful, but how do you shoot it? I move the camera in, it's dark, you can't see what the fuck's going on. Besides, you don't even want to see the guy. Leave him alone. I don't want to know him any more. Let me go home. I won't go see my pictures – that's a cute remark, but it's true. I haven't looked at it since I finished it. But when you came up with that masturbation idea at Musso-Frank's, I knew you understood something intrinsically, deep down. As you say, you deliver a structure and I put in detail, that kind of thing. But I need the structure, the direction. I eventually wound up going through my own personal crisis in a life and death situation; and when a friend, in the hospital, said, 'Do you really want to make this picture?' I found myself saying yes immediately, from my subconscious. Why? Because I understood that the character was no longer Jake, it was me, Bob, you, all of us. In structuring the film during that six weeks, you created a situation where I could understand the essence of it. Do you follow?

SCHRADER: But *Raging Bull* is not the film I wrote . . .

SCORSESE: Oh, but it is, my dear.

SCHRADER: *(Laughs)* OK.

SCORSESE: I've said this a number of times. I know we're a little tired and I hope you won't be offended, but when Brian De Palma gave me a copy of *Taxi Driver* and introduced us, I almost felt I wrote it myself. Not that I could write that way, but I felt everything. I was burning inside my fucking skin; I had to make it. And that's all there is to it, Paul, do you follow me?

SCHRADER: I know, and feel even stronger than you about it.

SCORSESE: Therefore there's something deeper than just paper between you and me. There's a man like that taxi driver, a man who is a fucking vehicle on screen.

SCHRADER: It's almost ten years later but I feel just as strong about *The Last Temptation of Christ (a script I was writing for Scorsese from the Nikos Kazantzakis's novel)*. It's the final panel of the triptych. No more middleweights; this time we'll deal with a heavyweight sufferer.

SCORSESE: You know, I like the script very much, and we're going to work on it, but I've got to take a rest after this picture . . .

SCHRADER: Of course you'll direct this. Because if you don't, I will – and you couldn't bear that!

SCORSESE: No, I couldn't deal with that at all. I really want to do it. I think I know what *he* looks like. A man in a tunic who says, 'Come over here, you're doing it all wrong.' It's a wonderful, wonderful idea. But I don't see it as middleweight or heavyweight. In the context of Christianity no person is minor league. Just as with Jake La Motta. Many critics said this animal, this Jake La Motta, judging from the film they judge the man! First, they have no right to judge the man. Second, they're dealing with an essence – like a whole tree distilled into one drop. And that something comes from me, you – it's so obvious it's ridiculous – and Bob. But Bob could never get himself into a situation like this, a philosophical discussion. Never. He was revealing himself in his own way. And that's why I like working with him.

SCHRADER: I'll make a generalization. Tell me what you think of it. The generalization is this: of the three films, I think *Taxi Driver* is more mine, *Raging Bull* more Bobby's, and *Last Temptation* will be more yours.

SCORSESE: It's a generalization; it's not true. Generalizations are not true. It's like looking at a marriage and saying he's right and she's wrong. She's always right, she's always wrong, he's always right. You can't go into somebody's marriage. And it's a marriage we're talking about.

SCHRADER: They are collaborations. Maybe I'm just saying the one originated with me, another with De Niro, another with you.

SCORSESE: And even that one, *Last Temptation*, was recommended to me by David Carradine and Barbara Hershey. Outsiders don't understand the collaborative process. I'm a writer and an actor too, but I don't take credit for writing. It doesn't matter. We all see if we can think of the same things in our own ways.

SCHRADER: When I was in Montreux I bought three stations of the cross which are hanging in my house. Each time I

xx

stumble drunkenly up the stairs I have to pass the stations of the cross. Do you still feel you're a Catholic?

SCORSESE: According to the Church?

SCHRADER: In the same way I'm a Protestant.

SCORSESE: I'm afraid so. We started talking about fulfilment. There's nothing worth anything else.

SCHRADER: What role does it play in your life?

SCORSESE: Are you talking about Mass, confession . . .?

SCHRADER: No, I guess I'm talking about private thoughts, imagery. What goes on when the lights go out.

SCORSESE: You fight the devil. That's not pretentious. You know what goes on when the lights go out? When I was having troubles, a black present fear of death, a depression from which I could not return and into which I was going deeper and deeper. There's got to be a way to stop that sort of thing. I do things to a bit of excess, I guess. The point is that after a certain age, and I'll be forty this year, certain things don't get you excited. When I was fifteen or sixteen this masturbation problem started in which I felt that I could kill myself slowly like Scobie in *Heart of the Matter* . . .

SCHRADER: *Jerusalem, Jerusalem* was the diary of a masturbator . . .

SCORSESE: Exactly. People say I'm a jerk-off. (*Laughs.*) The point is, you can't live with that guilt, you can't live with that guilt. Nine years of analysis. It's a matter of learning to deal with it. That's why I'm trying to redefine my life, editing this film, trying to keep a household together. I've moved from uptown to downtown – back to the old neighbourhood. It's a very difficult situation for me. I'm trying to hang in there. When I discovered masturbation, I was sure terrible things would happen to me. And sure enough they did. But terrible things happen every day – that's life. It's a matter of knowing what's good for yourself. It's a matter of working in your house, going downstairs to work, going back upstairs to sleep. Becoming a more and more compressed unit by yourself, being alone a lot of the time. It's a matter of overcoming that image of when life's gone. It's taken over the death image, thank God.

SCHRADER: This privilege we have as directors, creating fantasies . . .

SCORSESE: I can't do a fantasy. I can't create a fantasy. I don't believe that –

SCHRADER: OK, this privilege we have of creating unreal images, things that we make up, that never happened – does this privilege, this freedom, allow you to live vicariously? To what extent does it relieve sexual tension?

SCORSESE: None.

SCHRADER: I find the fantasy works.

SCORSESE: No.

SCHRADER: That leads me to my last question. This internal battle –

SCORSESE: This 'eternal bowel'?

SCHRADER: No, this *internal battle* –

SCORSESE: I'm sorry.

SCHRADER: This internal battle which expresses itself in your films – does it evolve or repeat?

SCORSESE: It repeats, but –

SCHRADER: Because if it only repeats . . .

SCORSESE: It repeats and evolves. We have to give each other strength. When you wrote *Last Temptation*, you gave me strength. But to put something on film doesn't mean you're rid of it. I was crazier when I finished *Taxi Driver* than when I began.

SCHRADER: It was just the opposite for me during the writing.

SCORSESE: There is an evolution. I've seen it. However, you also have patterns – and you have to deal with them.

SCHRADER: You're one of the few film-making friends I have left. I've dumped most of them because I don't feel they are growing. Their repetition, their stagnancy, is holding me back. So I let them go. But I don't think you have any choice but to grow. You couldn't choose not to grow.

SCORSESE: But when we do meet, it's like official meetings. We don't have any fucking social things. Do you know what I mean?

SCHRADER: Yes, it's sad.

'The whole conviction of my life now rests upon the belief that loneliness, far from being a rare and curious phenomenon, is the central and inevitable fact of human existence.'

Thomas Wolfe,
God's Lonely Man

Taxi Driver was released in 1976, winning the Palme d'Or at that year's Cannes Film Festival. The cast includes:

TRAVIS BICKLE	Robert De Niro
IRIS	Jodie Foster
BETSY	Cybill Shepherd
SPORT	Harvey Keitel
ANDY, the gun salesman	Steven Prince
TOM	Albert Brooks
WIZARD	Peter Boyle
CHARLES PALANTINE	Leonard Harris
Director	Martin Scorsese
Producers	Michael Phillips
	Julia Phillips
Cinematography	Michael Chapman
Editors	Marcia Lucas
	Tom Rolf
	Melvin Shapiro
Music	Bernard Hermann
Visual Consultant	David Nichols

Taxi Driver was released through Columbia Pictures.

TRAVIS BICKLE, *aged twenty-six, lean, hard, the consummate loner.*
On the surface he appears good-looking, even handsome; he has a
quiet steady look and a disarming smile which flashes from nowhere,
lighting up his whole face. But behind that smile, around his dark
eyes, in his gaunt cheeks, one can see the ominous strains caused by a
life of private fear, emptiness and loneliness. He seems to have
wandered in from a land where it is always cold, a country where
the inhabitants seldom speak. The head moves, the expression
changes, but the eyes remain ever-fixed, unblinking, piercing empty
space.
TRAVIS *is now drifting in and out of the New York City night life,*
a dark shadow among darker shadows. Not noticed, with no
reason to be noticed, TRAVIS *is one with his surroundings. He wears*
rider jeans, cowboy boots, a plaid western shirt and a worn beige
Army jacket with a patch reading 'King Kong Company,
1968–70'.
He has the smell of sex about him: sick sex, repressed sex, lonely
sex, but sex none the less. He is a raw male force, driving forward;
towards what, one cannot tell. Then one looks closer and sees the
inevitable. The clock spring cannot be wound continually tighter. As
the earth moves towards the sun, TRAVIS BICKLE *moves towards*
violence.

TRAVIS GETS A JOB

Film opens on exterior of Manhattan cab garage. Weather-beaten
sign above driveway reads, 'Taxi Enter Here'. Yellow cabs scuttle
in and out. It is winter, snow is piled on the kerbs, the wind is
howling.
Inside garage are parked row upon row of multi-coloured taxis.
Echoing sounds of cabs idling, cabbies talking. Steamy breath and
exhaust fill the air.
Corridor of cab company offices. Lettering on ajar door reads:

PERSONNEL OFFICE
Mavis Cab Company
Blue and White Cab Co.
Acme Taxi
Dependable Taxi Services
JRB Cab Company
Speedo Taxi Service

Sounds of office busy at work: shuffling, typing, arguing.
Personnel office is a cluttered disarray. Sheets with headings 'Mavis,
B&W, Acme' and so forth are tacked to crumbling plaster wall. It is
March. Desk is cluttered with forms, reports and an old upright
Royal typewriter.
Dishevelled middle-aged New Yorker looks up from the desk. We
cut in to ongoing conversation between the middle-aged PERSONNEL
OFFICER *and a young man standing in front of his desk.*
The young man is TRAVIS BICKLE. *He wears his jeans, boots and*
Army jacket. He takes a drag of his unfiltered cigarette.
The PERSONNEL OFFICER *is exhausted: he arrives at work*

exhausted. TRAVIS *is something else again. His intense steely gaze is enough to jar even the* PERSONNEL OFFICER *out of his workaday boredom.*

PERSONNEL OFFICER: (*Out of shot*) No trouble with the Hack Bureau?

TRAVIS: (*Out of shot*) No, sir.

PERSONNEL OFFICER: (*Out of shot*) Got your licence?

TRAVIS: (*Out of shot*) Yes.

PERSONNEL OFFICER: So why do you want to be a taxi-driver?

TRAVIS: I can't sleep nights.

PERSONNEL OFFICER: There's porno theatres for that.

TRAVIS: I know. I tried that.

(*The* PERSONNEL OFFICER, *though officious, is mildly probing and curious.* TRAVIS *is a cipher, cold and distant. He speaks as if his mind doesn't know what his mouth is saying.*)

PERSONNEL OFFICER: So what'ja do now?

TRAVIS: I ride around nights mostly. Subways, buses. See things. Figured I might as well get paid for it.

PERSONNEL OFFICER: We don't need any misfits around here, son.

(*A thin smile cracks almost indiscernably across* TRAVIS's *lips.*)

TRAVIS: You kiddin? Who else would hack through South Bronx or Harlem at night?

PERSONNEL OFFICER: *You* want to work uptown nights?

TRAVIS: I'll work anywhere, any time. I know I can't be choosy.

PERSONNEL OFFICER: (*Thinks a moment*) How's your driving record?

TRAVIS: Clean. Real clean. (*Pause, thin smile.*) As clean as my conscience.

PERSONNEL OFFICER: Listen, son, you gonna get smart, you can leave right now.

TRAVIS: (*Apologetic*) Sorry, sir. I didn't mean that.

PERSONNEL OFFICER: Physical? Criminal?

TRAVIS: Also clean.

PERSONNEL OFFICER: Age?

TRAVIS: Twenty-six.

PERSONNEL OFFICER: Education?

TRAVIS: Some. Here and there.

PERSONNEL OFFICER: Military record?

TRAVIS: Honourable discharge. May, 1971.

3

PERSONNEL OFFICER: You moonlightin'?

TRAVIS: No, I want long shifts.

PERSONNEL OFFICER: (*Casually, almost to himself*) We hire a lot of moonlighters here.

TRAVIS: So I hear.

PERSONNEL OFFICER: (*Looks up at* TRAVIS) Hell, we ain't that much fussy anyway. There's always openings on one fleet or another. (*Rummages through his drawer, collecting various pink, yellow and white forms.*) Fill out these forms and give them to the girl at the desk, and leave your phone number. You got a phone?

TRAVIS: No.

PERSONNEL OFFICER: Well then, check back tomorrow.

TRAVIS: Yes, sir.

(*Credits appear over scenes from Manhattan nightlife. The snow has melted; it is spring.*

A rainy, slick, wet, miserable night in Manhattan's theatre district. Cabs and umbrellas are congested everywhere; well-dressed pedestrians are pushing, running, waving down taxis. The high-class theatre patrons crowding out of the midtown shows are shocked to find that the same rain that falls on the poor and common is also falling on them.

The unremitting sounds of honking and shouting play against the dull pitter-patter of rain. The glare of yellow, red and green lights reflects off the pavements and autos.

'When it rains, the boss of the City is the taxi-driver' – so goes the cabbies' maxim, proved true by this particular night's activity. Only the taxis seem to rise above the situation: they glide effortlessly through the rain and traffic, picking up whom they choose, spurning whom they choose, going where they please.

Further uptown, the crowds are neither so frantic nor so glittering. The rain also falls on the street bums and the aged poor. Junkies still stand around on rainy street corners, hookers still prowl rainy sidewalks. And the taxis service them too.

All through the credits the exterior sounds are muted, as if coming from a distant room or storefront round the corner. The listener is at a safe but privileged distance.

After examining various strata of Manhattan nightlife, the

4

*camera begins to close in on one particular taxi, and it is
assumed that this taxi is being driven by* TRAVIS BICKLE.
The credits end.)

WE MEET TRAVIS

*Travis's yellow taxi pulls up in the foreground. On left rear door are
lettered the words 'Dependable Taxi Service'.*
*We are somewhere in the upper fifties on Fifth Avenue. The rain has
not let up.*
*An elderly woman climbs in the right rear door, crushing her
umbrella.* TRAVIS *waits a moment, then pulls away from the kerb
with a start.*
*Later, we see Travis's taxi speeding down the rain-slicked avenue.
The action is periodically accompanied by* TRAVIS'*s narration. He is
reading from a haphazard personal diary.*
TRAVIS: (*Voice over, monotone*) April 10, 1972. Thank God for
   the rain which has helped wash the garbage and trash off
   the sidewalks.
   (TRAVIS'*s point of view, of sleazy midtown side street: bums,
   hookers, junkies.*)
   I'm working a single now, which means stretch-shifts, six
   to six, sometimes six to eight in the a.m., six days a week.
   (*A* MAN IN BUSINESS SUIT *hails* TRAVIS *to the kerb.*)
   It's a hustle, but it keeps me busy. I can take in three to
   three-fifty a week, more with skims.
   (MAN IN BUSINESS SUIT, *now seated in back seat, speaks
   up.*)
MAN IN BUSINESS SUIT: (*Urgent*) Is Kennedy operating, cabbie?
   Is it grounded?
   (*On the seat next to* TRAVIS *is a half-eaten cheeseburger and
   order of french fries. He puts his cigarette down and gulps as he
   answers.*)
TRAVIS: Why should it be grounded?
MAN IN BUSINESS SUIT: Listen – I mean I just saw the needle
   of the Empire State Building. You can't see it for the fog!
TRAVIS: Then it's a good guess it's grounded.
MAN IN BUSINESS SUIT: The Empire State in fog means
   something, don't it? Do you know or don't you? What is
   your number, cabbie?

5

TRAVIS: Have you tried the telephone?

MAN IN BUSINESS SUIT: (*Hostile, impatient*) There isn't time for that. In other words, you don't know.

TRAVIS: No.

MAN IN BUSINESS SUIT: Well, you should know, damn it, or who else would know? Pull over right here. (*Points out of window.*) Why don't you stick your goddamn head out of the goddamn window once in a while and find out about the goddamn fog!

(TRAVIS *pulls to the kerb. The* MAN IN BUSINESS SUIT *stuffs a dollar bill into the pay drawer and jumps out of the cab. He turns to hail another taxi.*)

Taxi! Taxi!

(TRAVIS *writes up his trip card and drives away.*)

(*It is later that night. The rain has turned to drizzle.* TRAVIS *drives through another section of Manhattan.*)

TRAVIS: (*Voice over*) I work the whole city, up, down, don't make no difference to me – does to some.

(*Streetside:* TRAVIS's *point of view. Black* PROSTITUTE *wearing white vinyl boots, leopard-skin mini-skirt and blonde wig, hails taxi. On her arm hangs half-drunk seedy executive type.*

TRAVIS *pulls over.*

PROSTITUTE *and* JOHN (*the executive type*) *climb into back seat.* TRAVIS *checks out the action in rear-view mirror.*)

Some won't take spooks – Hell, don't make no difference to me.

(*Travis's taxi drives through Central Park.*

Grunts, groans coming from back seat. PROSTITUTE *and* JOHN *going at it in back seat. He's having a hard time and she's probably trying to get him to come off manually.*)

JOHN: (*Out of shot*) Oh baby, baby.

PROSTITUTE: (*Out of shot. Forceful*) Come on.

(TRAVIS *stares blankly ahead.*)

(*Travis's apartment. Camera pans silently across the interior, indicating this is not a new scene.*

TRAVIS *is sitting at plain table writing. He wears shirt, jeans, boots. An unfiltered cigarette rests in a bent coffee-can ashtray.*

Close-up of notebook. It is a plain lined dimestore notebook and the words TRAVIS *is writing with a stubby pencil are those he is saying. The columns are straight, disciplined. Some of the writing is in pencil, some in ink. The handwriting is jagged. Camera continues to pan, examining Travis's apartment. It is unusual, to say the least. A ratty old mattress is thrown against one wall. The floor is littered with old newspapers, worn and unfolded street maps and pornography. The pornography is of the sort that looks cheap but costs $10 a throw – black and white photos of naked women tied and gagged with black leather straps and clotheslines. There is no furniture other than the rickety chair and table. A beat-up portable TV rests on an upright melon-crate. The red silk mass in another corner looks like a Vietnamese flag. Indecipherable words, figures, numbers are scribbled on the plain plaster walls. Ragged black wires dangle from the wall where the telephone once hung.*)

TRAVIS: (*Voice over*) They're all animals anyway. All the animals come out at night: whores, skunk pussies, buggers, queens, fairies, dopers, junkies, sick, venal. (*A pause.*) Someday a *real* rain will come and wash all this scum off the streets.

(*Early morning, 6 a.m. The air is clean and fresh and the streets nearly deserted.*

Exterior of taxi garage. Travis's taxi pulls into the driveway.)

Each night when I return the cab to the garage I have to clean the come off the back seat. Some nights I clean off the blood.

(TRAVIS *pulls his taxi into taxi garage stall. He reaches across the cab and extracts a small vial of Bennies from the glove compartment.*

He stands next to the cab, straightens his back, and tucks the bottle of pills into his jacket pocket. He lowers his head, looks into back seat, opens rear door and bends inside. He shakes a cigarette out of his pack of Camels and lights it.

Slight timecut. TRAVIS *books in at garage office. Old, rotting slabs of wood are screwed to a grey crumbling concrete wall. Each available space is covered with hand-lettered signs, time schedules, check-out sheets, memos. The signs read:*

BE ALERT!
THE SANE DRIVER
IS ALWAYS READY
FOR THE UNEXPECTED

ALL NIGHT DRIVERS
HAVING PERSONAL INJURY
ACCIDENTS
MUST PHONE IN AT ONCE TO
JUDSON 2–3410
AND MUST FILE A REPORT *Promptly*
AT 9 AM THE FOLLOWING MORNING AT
43 W. 61ST.

SLOW DOWN
AND GAUGE SPEED TO
ROAD CONDITIONS
YOU CAN'T STOP
ON A DIME!

A half-dozen haggard cabbies hang around the office. Their shirts are wrinkled, their heads dropping, their mouths incessantly chattering. We pick up snatches of cabbie small talk.)

FIRST CABBIE: . . . hadda piss like a bull steer, so I pull over on 10th Ave, yank up the hood and do the engine job. (*Gestures as if taking a piss into the hood*) There I am with my dong in my hand when a guy come up and asks if I need any help. 'Just checking the battery,' I says, and, meanwhile . . . (*Takes imaginary piss.*)

SECOND CABBIE: If he thinks I'm going up into The Jungle this time of night, he can shove it.

THIRD CABBIE: (*Talking into pay-phone*) Fuck that Violets First. Fucking saddle horse. No, no, the OTB. Fuck them. No, it was TKR. TCR and I'da made seven fucking grand. Fuck them too. All right, what about the second race?

FOURTH CABBIE: Over at Love, this hooker took on the whole garage. Blew the whole fucking joint and they wouldn't even let her use the drinking fountain.

(TRAVIS *hands his trip sheet to the cab official, nods slightly, turns and walks towards the door.*

Outside, TRAVIS *walks pleasantly down Broadway, his hands*

8

in his jacket pockets. The sidewalks are deserted, except for diligent fruit and vegetable vendors setting up their stalls. He takes a deep breath of fresh air, pulls a white pill from his pocket, pops it into his mouth.

He turns a corner, keeps walking. Ahead of him is a twenty-four-hour porno theatre. The theatre, a blaze of cheap Day-Glo reds and yellows, is an offence to the clear, crisp morning air. The permanent lettering reads, 'Adam Theater. 16 mm Sound Features'. Underneath, today's features are hand-lettered: 'Six-Day Cruise' and 'Beaver Dam'. TRAVIS *stops at the box office, purchases a ticket, and walks in.*)

(Porno theatre.
Inside the porno theatre, TRAVIS *stands in the aisle for a moment. He turns round, walking back towards the concession stand.*

A plain, dumpy-looking GIRL *sits listlessly on a stool behind the shabby concession stand. A plaster-of-paris Venus de Milo sits atop a piece of purple velvet cloth on the counter. The sound of the feature drones in the background.*)

CONCESSIONS GIRL: Kin I help ya?
    (TRAVIS *rests his elbow on the counter, looking at the* GIRL. *He is obviously trying to be friendly – no easy task for him. God knows he needs a friend.*)

TRAVIS: What is your name? My name is Travis.
CONCESSIONS GIRL: Awh, come off it, pal.
TRAVIS: No, I'm serious, really . . .
CONCESSIONS GIRL: Ya want me to call da boss? Huh? That what you want?
TRAVIS: No, no, it's all right. I'll have a big Coca-Cola – without ice – and a large buttered popcorn, and . . . (*Pointing*) some of them chocolate covered malted milk balls . . . and ju-jukes, a box. They last.
CONCESSIONS GIRL: We don't have ju-jukes. We don't have Coca-Cola. We only got Royal Crown Cola.
TRAVIS: That's fine.
CONCESSIONS GIRL: That's a dollar forty-seven.
    (TRAVIS *lays two dollar bills on the counter.*)

(Inside the theatre auditorium.

9

Slight timecut. TRAVIS *is sitting in theatre, drinking his Royal Crown Cola, eating his popcorn and milk balls. His eyes are fixed on the screen. A* MALE VOICE *emanates from the screen.*)

MALE MOVIE VOICE: (*Out of shot*) Come here, bitch. I'm gonna split you in half.

(MOVIE VOICE *yields to* TRAVIS's *monotone narration.*)

TRAVIS: (*Voice over*) Twelve hours of work and I still cannot sleep. The days dwindle on for ever and do not end.

WE MEET BETSY

Exterior of Charles Palantine campaign headquarters.
The headquarters of the 'New Yorkers for Charles Palantine for President Committee', located at the corner of 58th Street and Broadway, are festooned in traditional red, white and blue banners, ribbons and signs.
One large sign proclaims 'Palantine'. Another sign reads 'Register for New York Primary, July 20'. The smiling middle-aged face of Charles Palantine keeps watch over the bustling pedestrians.
It is late afternoon.
Inside headquarters, a variety of young workers joke and chatter as they labour through stacks of papers. The room is pierced with the sound of ringing phones.
Seen from a distance – the only way TRAVIS *can see them – these are America's chosen youth: healthy, energetic, well-groomed, attractive, all recruited from the bucolic fields of Massachusetts and Connecticut.*
The camera favours BETSY, *about twenty-five, an extremely attractive woman sitting at the reception desk between two phones and several stacks of papers. Her attractions, however, are more than skin deep. Beneath that Cover Girl facial there is a keen, though highly specialized, sensibility: her eyes scan every man who passes her desk as her mind computes his desirability: political, intellectual, sexual, emotional, material. Simple pose and status do not impress her; she seeks out the extraordinary qualities in men. She is, in other words, a star-fucker of the highest order.*
BETSY, *putting down the phone, calls* TOM, *a lanky, amiable and modishly long-haired campaign worker, over to her desk.*
BETSY: Tom.

(TOM *is pleasant and good-looking, but lacks those special*

qualities which interest BETSY. *He gets nowhere with* BETSY –
*yet he keeps trying. Just another of those routine office
flirtations which pass the hours and free the fantasies.*)

BETSY: Tom, come here a moment.

(*He walks over.*)

I think this canvas report is about ready to go out. Check it
out with Andy, and if he okays it, have a copy made for the
campaign headquarters in every county. (*Pause.*) And don't
forget to add the new photo releases.

TOM: The senator's White Paper is almost ready, Bets. Should
we wait for that?

BETSY: Andy usually just sends those to the national media. The
local press doesn't know what to do with a position paper
until UPI and AP tell them anyway.

TOM: I think we should try to get maximum coverage for this
new mandatory welfare programme. Push the issue.

BETSY: (*As if instructing a child*) First push the man, then the
issue. Senator Palantine is first of all a dynamic man, an
intelligent, interesting, fascinating man.

TOM: You forgot 'sexy'.

BETSY: No, I didn't forget 'sexy'.

TOM: Just didn't get around to it, huh?

BETSY: Oh, Tom, please.

TOM: Well, for Christsakes, you sound like you're selling . . . I
don't know what . . . cars . . . not issues.

BETSY: Have you ever wondered why CBS News has the highest
ratings?

TOM: More people watch it.

BETSY: All right, forget it if you're not going to be serious.

TOM: No, c'mon, I'm listening. I was just . . .

BETSY: Just what?

TOM: Kidding around . . . you know, fun.

(BETSY *looks towards the street, then back at* TOM.)

BETSY: Maybe if you'd try thinking once in a while, you'd get
somewhere.

TOM: With who?

BETSY: All right, now. You want to know why CBS has the
highest ratings? You think their news is any different from
NBC, ABC? It's all the same news. Same stories. Same

order usually. What, you thought they had good news for people, right? You thought that's why people watched CBS? I'll tell you why people watch CBS. Cronkite. The man. You got it? Not the news, not the issues, the man. If Walter Cronkite told people to eat soap, they'd do it. We *are* selling cars, goddamn it.

(BETSY's *attention is being distracted by something she sees across the street. She puts on her glasses and looks out across the street again.*)

TOM: Well, if Cronkite's so great, why don't we run *him* instead?

BETSY: That's the last. The finish. Period. Some people can learn. Some people can't. And you wonder why we never get serious –

TOM: Sure we could run him. You realize he's already president of his block association?

BETSY: (*Looks across street again*) Have you been noticing anything strange?

TOM: No, why?

BETSY: Why's that taxi-driver across the street been staring at us?

TOM: What taxi-driver?

BETSY: *That* taxi-driver. The one that's been sitting there.

TOM: How long has he been there?

BETSY: I don't know – but it feels like a long time.

(TRAVIS's *cold, piercing eyes stare out from his cab, parked across the street from the Palantine headquarters. He is like a lone wolf watching the warm camp fires of civilization from a distance. A thin red dot glows from his cigarette.* TOM *exchanges* TRAVIS's *gaze.*)

TOM: (*Determined*) Well, I'll go out and ask him.

(As TOM *walks towards the front door,* BETSY's *eyes alternate between him and the position where* TRAVIS *sits.*

TOM *strides out the front door and walks briskly out of the Palantine headquarters, across the street towards Travis's taxi.*

TRAVIS *spots* TOM *walking towards him and quickly starts up his cab, then squeals off in a burst of billowing exhaust.*

TOM *watches the speeding taxi quizzically.*

Travis's taxi continues down Broadway.)

Inside Travis's apartment.
TRAVIS *lies on his mattress, staring at the ceiling. He is fully clothed and appears deep in thought.*
Near his mattress rest several medications: a large bottle of vitamin pills, two smaller bottles of pills, a bottle of peach-flavoured brandy.
TRAVIS: (*Voice over*) All my life needed was a sense of direction, a sense of someplace to go. I do not believe one should devote his life to morbid self-attention, but should become a person like other people.
(*Another day. Late afternoon.*
Travis's taxi is driving down Broadway with the 'Off Duty' sign on.
Tracking shot down Broadway. Camera stops at Palantine campaign headquarters. A few workers remain in the office. Betsy's desk is vacant.)
(*Fifth Avenue. The same afternoon.*
Camera tracks with crowded mass of Manhattanites as they ooze through the sidewalks towards their various destinations. Individuals are indiscernible: it is simply a congested mass.)
I first saw her at Palantine Campaign Headquarters at 58th and Broadway. She was wearing a yellow dress, answering the phone at her desk.
(*Suddenly: out of the congested human mass, in slowing motion, appears the slender figure of* BETSY, *in a stylish yellow dress. The crowd parts like the Red Sea, and there she is: walking all alone, untouched by the crowd, suspended in space and time.*)
She appeared like an angel out of this open sewer. Out of this filthy mass. She is alone: they cannot touch her.
(*Inside Travis's apartment.*
TRAVIS *is at the table, writing in his diary.*
Close-up: his stubby pencil rests on the word 'her'.)

SMALL TALK IN A GREASY SPOON

It is 3.30 in the morning in a bacon-shaped all-night West Side restaurant. The thick smell hangs in the air – fried grease, smoke, sweat, regurgitated wine.

Whatever doesn't flush away in New York at night turns up in places like this. A burly grease-stained cook stands over the grill. A junkie shuffles from one side of the door to another. Slouched over the small four-person formica tables are several well-dressed blacks (too well-dressed for this time and place), a cluster of street people and a lost old coot who hangs on to his cup of coffee as if it were his last possession.

The restaurant, brightly lit, perfectly conveys the image of urban plasticity – without the slightest hint of an accompanying cleanliness. Toward the rear of the restaurant sit three cabbies: WIZARD, *a worn man of about fifty,* DOUGH-BOY, *younger family man,* CHARLIE T, *fortyish, black.*

WIZARD *is telling* DOUGH-BOY *a story.* CHARLIE T, *his elbows propped against the table top, is not listening. He stares silently down at a plate of cold scrambled eggs and a* Racing Forum. *His eyes may not be open.*

WIZARD: First she did her make-up. You know, I hate it when
    they do that. I mean she does the whole works, the
    mascara, the eye-shadow, the lipstick, the rouge . . .
DOUGH-BOY: Not rouge. Blush-On, they call it.
WIZARD: The kind with a brush?
    (TRAVIS *appears at the door. He has to push aside the junkie in*
    order to enter, without making physical contact – something
    TRAVIS *would not relish. He may be repulsed with these people*
    and this place, but he is too much a part of this to let his
    feelings rise to the surface.
    WIZARD *gives* TRAVIS *a perfunctory wave.*)
WIZARD: Travis.
TRAVIS: Hey Wizard.
    (TRAVIS *straddles a seat at the table.* DOUGH-BOY *gives*
    TRAVIS *something between a wink and an eye-twitch and says:*)
DOUGH-BOY: Yeah, that's Blush-On. My wife uses it.
WIZARD: (*Ironic*) Ask Travis. He's the ladies' man.
    (TRAVIS *shrugs and motions for a cup of coffee.*)
    Well, whatever the fuck it is, she used it. And then the
    spray perfume. You know, the real sweet kind – and, on
    top of that, get this, right when we're crossing the Tri-boro
    bridge – she changes her pantyhose!
DOUGH-BOY: No.
    (TRAVIS *turns his head. He appears not be interested, but is.*)

WIZARD: Yeah.

DOUGH-BOY: Could you see anything?

WIZARD: Well, she was trying to keep her skirt down, sort of, you know. But it was pretty obvious what she was doing. I mean, Christ, it was rush hour and the traffic's practically standing still.

DOUGH-BOY: What did you do?

WIZARD: Threw on the emergency, jumped the seat and fucked her brains out – what do you think! (*They laugh.*) What do I have to do? Draw you a picture?

DOUGH-BOY: Yeah.

WIZARD: What was I supposed to do? I was watching in the rear-view. You know, just checkin' traffic.

DOUGH-BOY: She saw you watching?

(*A waitress brings Travis's coffee and a glass of water. He asks for a cheeseburger.*)

WIZARD: Sure. What do you think? She wanted to get out of the cab. I said, 'Look, you're in the middle of the fucking bridge . . .'

DOUGH-BOY: You said that? You said 'fuckin'' to her?

WIZARD: Well, I said, 'Lady, please, we're on a bridge . . .'

DOUGH-BOY: And what happened?

(TRAVIS *awaits* WIZARD'*s answer.*)

WIZARD: She stayed in the cab, what's she gonna do? But she stiffed me. A real skunk.

DOUGH-BOY: A real skunk.

(WIZARD *realizes* TRAVIS *and* DOUGH-BOY *may not have met.*)

WIZARD: (*Paternal*) Travis, you know Dough-Boy, Charlie T?

(CHARLIE T *nods sleepily.* TRAVIS *indicates he knows* DOUGH-BOY.)

DOUGH-BOY: Yeah. We went to Harvard together. (*Laughs.*)

WIZARD: We call him Dough-Boy cause he likes the dollars. He'll chase a buck straight into Jersey.

DOUGH-BOY: Look who's talking? (*Gestures around table.*) Who else would stay up all night to catch the morning rush hour?

(TRAVIS *sips his coffee.* CHARLIE T'*s eyelids slip shut.*)

WIZARD: (*To Travis*) So how'sit?

15

TRAVIS: (*In a monotone*) Some fleet driver for Bell just got cut up. Just heard it on the radio.

DOUGH-BOY: Stick up?

TRAVIS: No, just some crazy fucker. Cut half his ear off.

DOUGH-BOY: Where?

TRAVIS: In the Jungle. 122nd.

(TRAVIS's *eyes turn towards the restaurant's other patrons. There are three street people sitting at a table. One guy, stoned, stares straight ahead. A raggedly attractive girl rests her head on the shoulder of the other, a heavily bearded young man with a headband. They kiss and tease each other, momentarily lost in their separate world.*

TRAVIS *watches the hippie couple closely, his feelings sharply divided between cultural contempt and morose jealousy. Why should these people enjoy the love and intimacy that has always eluded him? He must enjoy these schizoid emotions, because his eyes dwell on the couple.*)

DOUGH-BOY: (*Out of shot, changing the subject*) You run all over town, don't you, Travis?

WIZARD: (*Referring to 122nd St*) Fuckin' Mau Mau land, that's what it is.

(TRAVIS *turns back to his companions.*)

TRAVIS: Huh?

DOUGH-BOY: I mean, you handle some pretty rough traffic, huh?

TRAVIS: (*Catching on*) I have.

DOUGH-BOY: You carry a piece? You need one?

TRAVIS: Nah. (*Pause.*) I suppose not.

(*The waitress slaps down a smudge-marked glass of water, and a cheeseburger plate that looks more like a shrunken head on a serving platter.*)

DOUGH-BOY: Well, you ever need one, I know a feller that kin getcha a real nice deal. Lotsa shit around.

WIZARD: The cops and company raise hell if they find out.

(TRAVIS *drops two Alka-Seltzers into his glass of water.*)

DOUGH-BOY: Truck drivers bring up Harlem Specials that blow up in your hand. But this guy don't deal no shit. Just quality. If you ever need anything, I can put you in touch.

WIZARD: For a fee.

DOUGH-BOY: For a fee.

16

WIZARD: I never use mine. But it's a good thing to have. Just as a threat.

DOUGH-BOY: (*Getting up*) Well, if there's this many hackies *inside*, there must be lots of fares *outside*. And I'm gonna go hustle 'em.

WIZARD: What ya gonna do with all that money, Dough-Boy?

DOUGH-BOY: Support my kids. Can you dig it? (*Pause.*) Nice to meet ya, Travis. So long, Wizard. (*Nods to* CHARLIE T.) Say hello to Malcolm X for me.

(CHARLIE T *remains unmoved: he is sleeping.*

DOUGH-BOY *exits.* TRAVIS *smiles perfunctorily, then looks back at* WIZARD. *They really don't have much to talk about, and the* WIZARD *doesn't care to manufacture any more conversation.*

TRAVIS *scans the greasy spoon: the scene is unchanged.*)

BETSY MEETS TRAVIS BICKLE

Exterior of the Palantine headquarters – another day. Traffic passes. Inside the Palantine headquarters. TOM *and* BETSY *are talking. She takes out a cigarette. He takes out matches to light it.*

BETSY: Try holding the match like this.

TOM: This has gotta be a game, right?

BETSY: (*Putting on her glasses*) This I gotta see.

TOM: (*Burning fingers*) Ouch!

BETSY: (*Giggling*) Oh, are you all right?

TOM: I'm great. Always set my fingers on fire. Nothing to it. Want to see another trick? I do this thing with my nose.

BETSY: No. I just wanted to see if you could light it that way. The guy at the news-stand can.

TOM: Ah, yes, the guy at the news-stand, Mr Asbestos . . .

BETSY: He happens to be missing fingers. I first noticed when –

TOM: Is he Italian?

BETSY: No, why?

TOM: You sure he's not Italian?

BETSY: He's *black*, OK?

TOM: Well, if he had been Italian, they could have been shot off. Sometimes the mob does that to teach guys a lesson. If they blow a job or something.

BETSY: As I said, he isn't Italian. Besides, I thought they just killed them.

TOM: Don't be naïve. They can't kill everybody. They have different punishments for different things. Like, if they kill a stool pigeon, they leave a canary on the body. It's symbolic.

BETSY: Why don't they leave a pigeon instead of a canary?

TOM: I don't know. Maybe they don't leave a canary. Don't be technical. What I'm saying is if this news-stand guy's Italian and his fingers are gone, maybe he's a thief.

BETSY: First, he's not Italian. Second, he's not a thief. I noticed the fingers when he was getting my change – the right change. Two of his fingers are missing. Just stubs. Like they were blown away. I was putting my change in my purse when I saw him get out a cigarette. I couldn't help watching. I was dying to see how he'd light it.

TOM: With the other hand, right?

BETSY: No, stupid. With the stubs. That's the whole point.

TOM: I know that guy. His hand looks like a paw. An old black guy, the news-stand at –

BETSY: No, this is young – well, I'm never sure how old black
people are – but, anyway, he isn't old. That's for sure.
TOM: Show me how he did that again.

(*Across the street from the headquarters.*
TRAVIS *is striding briskly across Broadway towards the
Palantine headquarters.*
*He is dressed the best we have seen him: his trousers (not jeans)
are pressed, his boots shined, his hair combed. Under his Army
jacket he wears a freshly laundered shirt and Ivy League tie.*
He drops his cigarette, steps on it and walks in.
Watching TRAVIS *enter Palantine's headquarters, we are again
surprised to realize that* TRAVIS *is really quite attractive. His
deformities are psychological, not physical. He believes he is
cursed, and therefore he is.*
TRAVIS *walks briskly into the office, and heads towards Betsy's
desk.* TOM *walks over to greet him, but* TRAVIS *ignores him.*)
TRAVIS: (*At Betsy's desk*) I want to volunteer.
(*As the camera examines* TRAVIS's *face more closely, one can
see the hollowness wrought by lack of sleep and an insufficient
diet.*)
TOM: (*Interrupting*) If you'll come this way.
(TRAVIS *elbows* TOM *off.*)
TRAVIS: (*To* BETSY) No. I want to volunteer to *you*.
TOM: (*Under his voice*) Bets.
(BETSY *waves* TOM *off with a short gesture, indicating
everything is OK. He walks away.*)
BETSY: (*Curious*) And why is that?
(TRAVIS *is on his best behaviour. He smiles slightly.*)
TRAVIS: Because you are the most beautiful woman I have ever
seen.
(BETSY *is momentarily taken back, but pleased.* TRAVIS's
presence has a definite sexual charge. He has those star qualities
BETSY *looks for: she senses there is something special about the
young man who stands before her. And then, too, there is that
disarming smile. He is, as* BETSY *would say, 'fascinating'.*)
BETSY: (*Smiling*) Is that so? (*Pause.*) But what do you think of
Charles Palantine?
TRAVIS: (*His mind elsewhere*) Who, Ma'am?

BETSY: Charles Palantine. The man you want to volunteer to help elect President.

TRAVIS: Oh, I think he's a wonderful man. Make a great, great President.

BETSY: You want to canvass?

TRAVIS: Yes, Ma'am.

(BETSY *is interviewing* TRAVIS, *but she is also teasing him a little, leading him on in a gentle feminine way*.)

BETSY: How do you feel about Senator Palantine's stand on welfare?

(*This takes* TRAVIS *back a bit. He obviously doesn't have the slightest idea what Palantine's stand on welfare is; in fact, he doesn't have any ideas about politics whatsoever.* TRAVIS *thinks a moment, then improvises an answer*.)

TRAVIS: Welfare, Ma'am? I think the Senator's right. People should work for a living. I do. Every day. I like to work. Get those old coots off welfare and make 'em work for a change.

(BETSY *does a subtle double-take: this isn't exactly Palantine's position on welfare. She remains intrigued by* TRAVIS.)

BETSY: Well, that's not exactly what the Senator has proposed. You might not want to canvass, but there is plenty of other work we need done: office work, filing, poster hanging.

TRAVIS: I'm a good worker, Betsy Ma'am, a real good worker.

BETSY: (*Gesturing*) If you talk to Tom, he'll assign you to something.

TRAVIS: If you don't mind, Ma'am, I'd rather work for you.

BETSY: Well, we're *all* working tonight.

TRAVIS: Well, Betsy Ma'am, I drive a taxi at night.

BETSY: Well, then, what is it you *exactly* want to do?

TRAVIS: (*Bolstering courage*) If you don't mind, Ma'am, I'd be mighty pleased if you'd go out and have some coffee and pie with me.

(BETSY *doesn't quite know what to make of* TRAVIS. *She is curious, intrigued, tantalized. Like a moth, she draws closer to the flame*.)

BETSY: Why?

TRAVIS: Well, Betsy Ma'am, I drive by this place here in my taxi many times a day. And I watch you sitting here at this big long desk with these telephones, and I say to myself, that's a lonely girl. She needs a friend. And I'm gonna be her friend. (*Smiles.*)

(TRAVIS *rarely smiles, but when he does his whole face glows. It is as if he is able to tap an inner reserve of charm unknown even to himself.* BETSY *is completely disarmed.*)

BETSY I don't know . . .

TRAVIS: It's just to the corner, Ma'am. In broad daytime. Nothing can happen. I'll be there to protect you.

BETSY: (*Smiles, relenting*) All right. All right. I'm taking a break at four o'clock. If you're here then we'll go to the corner and have some coffee and pie.

TRAVIS: Oh, I appreciate that, Betsy Ma'am. I'll be here at four o'clock exactly. (*Pause.*) And . . . ah . . . Betsy . . .

BETSY: Yes?

TRAVIS: My name is Travis.

BETSY: Thank you, Travis.

(TRAVIS *nods, turns and exits.*

TOM, *who has been watching this interchange with a pseudo-standoffish (actually jealous) air, steps over to* BETSY. *His manner demands some sort of explanation of what she was doing.*

BETSY *simply shrugs – it's really none of his business.*)

BETSY: I'm just going to find out what the cabbies are thinking.

COFFEE-SHOP RENDEZVOUS

TRAVIS *is pacing back and forth on Broadway just beyond the Palantine headquarters. He checks his watch.*

TRAVIS: (*Voice over*) April 26, 1972. Four o'clock p.m. I took Betsy to the Mayfair coffee shop on Broadway . . .

(TRAVIS *and* BETSY *are sitting in a booth of a small New York coffee shop. They have both been served coffee;* TRAVIS *is nervously turning his cup around in his hands.*

The waitress brings their orders: apple pie for TRAVIS, *fruit compote for* BETSY.)

I had black coffee and apple pie with a slice of melted yellow cheese. I think that was a good selection. Betsy had coffee and a fruit salad dish. She could have had anything she wanted.

(BETSY'S *conversation interrupts* TRAVIS.)

BETSY: We've signed up 15,000 Palantine volunteers in New York so far. The organizational problems are becoming just staggering.

TRAVIS: I know what you mean. I've got the same problems. I just can't get things organized. Little things, I mean. Like my room, my possessions. I should get one of those signs that says, 'One of These Days I'm Gonna Get Organezizied.' (TRAVIS *contorts his mouth to match his mispronunciation, then breaks into a big, friendly, infectious grin. The very sight of it makes one's heart pound.*

BETSY *cannot help but be caught up in* TRAVIS's *grin.*
TRAVIS's *contagious, quicksilver moods cause her to say:*)
BETSY: (*Laughing*) Travis, I never ever met *any*body like you before.
TRAVIS: I can believe that.
BETSY: Where *do* you live?
TRAVIS: (*Evasive*) Oh, uptown. You know. Some joint. It ain't much.
BETSY: So why did you decide to drive a taxi at *night*?
TRAVIS: I had a regular job for a while, days. You know, doin' this, doin' that. But I didn't have anything to do at *night*. I got kinda lonely, you know, just wanderin' around. So I decided to work nights. It ain't good to be alone, you know.
BETSY: After this job, I'm looking *forward* to being alone for a while.
TRAVIS: Yeah, well . . . (*Pause*.) In a cab you get to meet people. You meet lots a' people. It's good for you.
BETSY: What kind of people?
TRAVIS: Just people people, you know. Just people. (*Pause*.) Had a dead man once.
BETSY: Really?
TRAVIS: He'd been shot. I didn't know that. He just crawled into the back seat, said 'West 45th Street' and conked out.
BETSY: What did you do?
TRAVIS: I shut the meter off, for one thing. I knew I wasn't going to get paid. Then I dropped him off at the cop shop. They took him.
BETSY: That's really something.
TRAVIS: Oh, you see lots of freaky stuff in a cab. Especially when the moon's out.
BETSY: The moon?
TRAVIS: The full moon. One night I had three or four weirdos in a row and I looked up and, sure enough, there it was – the full moon.
(BETSY *laughs*.)
Oh, yeah. People will do anything in front of a taxi driver. I mean *anything*. People too cheap to rent a hotel room, people scoring dope, people shooting up, people who want

23

to embarrass you. (*A bitterness emerges.*) It's like you're not even there, not even a person. Nobody knows you.

(BETSY *cuts* TRAVIS's *bitterness short.*)

BETSY: Com'on, Travis. It's not that bad. I take lots of taxis.

TRAVIS: I know. I could have picked you up.

BETSY: Huh?

TRAVIS: Late one night. About three. At the Plaza.

BETSY: Three in the morning? I don't think so. I have to go to bed early. I work *days*. It must have been somebody else.

TRAVIS: No. It was you. You had some manila folders and a pink bag from Saks.

(BETSY, *realizing* TRAVIS *remembers her precisely, scrambles for a polite rationale for her behaviour.*)

BETSY: You're right! Now I remember! It was after the Western regional planners were in town and the meeting went on late. The next day I was completely bushed. It was unbelievable.

TRAVIS: If it wasn't for a drunk I would have picked you up. He wanted to go to the DMZ.

BETSY: The DMZ?

TRAVIS: South Bronx. The worst. I tried to ditch him, but he was already in the cab, so I had to take him. That's the law. Otherwise I would have picked you up.

BETSY: That would have been quite a coincidence.

TRAVIS: You'd be surprised how often you see the same people, get the same fare. People have patterns. They do more or less the same things every day. I can tell.

BETSY: Well, I don't go to the Plaza every night.

TRAVIS: I didn't mean you. But just ordinary people. A guy I know – Dough-Boy – met his wife that way. They got to talking. She said she usually caught the bus so he started picking her up at the bus stop, taking her home with the flag up.

BETSY: That's very romantic. Some of your fares must be interesting. See any stars, politicians, deliver any babies yet?

TRAVIS: (*Embarrassed*) Well, no . . . not really . . . had some famous people in the cab . . . (*Remembering*) I got this guy who makes lasers. Not regular lasers, not the big kind. Little lasers, pocket-sized, small enough to clip to your belt

like a transistor radio, like a gun, you know. Like a ray
gun. Zap.
BETSY: (*Laughs*) What hours *do* you work?
TRAVIS: I work a single, which means there's no replacement –
no second man on the cab. Six to six, sometimes eight.
Seventy-two hours a week.
BETSY: (*Amazed*) You mean you work seventy-two hours a
week?
TRAVIS: Sometimes seventy-six or eighty. Sometimes I squeeze a
few more hours in the morning. Eighty miles a day, a
hundred miles a night.
BETSY: You must be rich.
TRAVIS: (*Big affectionate smile*) It keeps ya busy.
BETSY: You know what you remind me of?
TRAVIS: What?
BETSY: That song by Kris Kristofferson, where it says 'he's a
prophet and a pusher, partly truth, partly fiction, a walking
contradiction'. (*Smiles.*)
TRAVIS: (*Uneasy*) I'm no pusher, Betsy. Honest. I never have
pushed.
BETSY: I didn't mean that, Travis. Just the part about the
contradiction.
TRAVIS: (*More at ease*) Oh. Who was that again?
BETSY: The singer?
TRAVIS: Yeah. I don't follow music too much.
BETSY: (*Slowly*) Kris Kristofferson.
  (TRAVIS *looks at* BETSY *intently and they exchange smiles.*)

INCIDENT IN A RECORD SHOP

TRAVIS *is walking confusedly around Sam Goody's at midday,
obviously unable to locate what he desires.*
*He is lost among the hip, young intellectual types that populate the
store. He watches the stylish, attractive female assistant, unable to
come right out and request what he desires.*
*A young sales girl sees his plight, walks over and asks if he needs
any help.* TRAVIS *inaudibly says a name to her, although the name
is obviously Kristofferson's.*
The sales girl digs out Kristofferson's Silver-Tongued Devil *album
for him.*

TRAVIS *says something else to the sales girl and she goes off to gift-wrap the album.*
TRAVIS *emerges from the record store, the brightly gift-wrapped album proudly tucked under his arm.*

A NIGHT BEHIND THE WHEEL

A lengthy point-of-view-shot from TRAVIS's *vantage-point behind the wheel.*
We see the city as TRAVIS *sees it. The front windscreen is a little dirty, the lit-up meter juts up at the lower right screen. The intercom crackles with static and messages.*
The lights turn green; we take off with a start. A short first gear – quick shift – a long second gear. The cab eases to the right of the street, checking out prospective fares.
Our eyes scan the long line of pedestrians. The regulars – bums, junkies, tourists, hookers, homosexuals, hippies – they mean nothing now. They only blend into the sidewalks and lighted storefronts.
Our eyes now concentrate on those that step away from the kerb – is that man hailing a cab or scratching his head?
In the next block there are perhaps three, four fares – quick gas-up through this yellow light – brake sharply – check the action. The first: tourists, nickel tippers – let the next guy pick them up. Let the second go also, the third – there's a live fare: a middle-aged local woman, short fare to the East Side, good tip.
We pull over to the kerb, waiting for her to get in. It is a long wait – a black streetwalker crosses in front of the cab. We focus on (as TRAVIS *would) a young couple embracing in the distance.*
As we travel, we hear TRAVIS's *random thoughts about selecting fares and tips.*
TRAVIS: (*Voice over*) You work at night, you get an instinct. You can smell them. The big tippers, the stiffs, the trouble makers. Quarter is good tip for Manhattan. Queens is better, Brooklyn the best. Go for the guy with suitcases. The rich are the worst tippers, Hooks are lousy. Spooks are OK, but they don't live on Park Avenue, after all.
(*The meter is activated: $0.60 registers. Tick, tick, tick. A quick glance shows the woman is now seated. She says softly, '192 East 89'. We take off with another jolt. Cross back up 9th Avenue, then cut through the park.*

We're zooming up 9th Avenue; how many green lights can we string together? Somebody steps out to hail the cab, but quickly steps back again. The meter is up to $0.90. It'll be a $1.40 fare.

Now through the park and we're almost there. Check the numbers – 134 – 140. End of the block. The fare comes to $1.40.

Check back mirror – she's getting out two bills. Two quarters and a dime change. Tip'll be either 0.25 or 0.35.

The tip comes back: 35c; a good tip. Good lady. We take off again with a jolt.

This is TRAVIS's *world: dark side streets, garish glaring main streets, quick glances, quicker evaluations – a dozen instantaneous decisions a minute. Are these people, are these objects?*

Travis's taxi speeds down a darkened street.

TRAVIS *lets off a fare and pulls into line at the Plaza.*)

TRAVIS: (*Voice over*) I called Betsy again at her office, and she said maybe we could go to a movie together after she gets off work tomorrow. That's my day off. At first she hesitated, but I called her again and she agreed. (*Pause.*) Betsy. Betsy what? I forgot to ask her last name again. Damn. I've got to remember stuff like that.

(TRAVIS's *thoughts are with* BETSY *as three men enter Travis's cab. He activates the meter and pulls off.*)

MAN: (*Out of shot*) St Regis Hotel.

(TRAVIS *checks the mirror. Scanning across the back seat, he recognizes the middle passenger. It is* CHARLES PALANTINE, *candidate for President. He must have left the hotel shortly after* BETSY.

TOM, *seated on the jump seat, checks his watch and speaks deferentially to* PALANTINE.)

TOM: It's 12.30 now. You'll have fifteen minutes before the actual luncheon begins.

(PALANTINE *nods as his* ASSISTANT *picks up the thread of an earlier conversation.*)

ASSISTANT: I don't think we have to worry about anybody here committing themselves until things start coming in from California.

(TRAVIS *puts out his cigarette.*)

TRAVIS: (*Interrupting*) Say, aren't you Charles Palantine, the candidate?

PALANTINE: (*Only mildly irritated*) Yes, I am.

TRAVIS: Well, I'm one of your biggest supporters, I tell everybody that comes in this cab that they should vote for you.

PALANTINE: (*Pleased; glances to check Travis's licence*) Why, thank you Travis.

TRAVIS: I'm sure you'll win, sir. Everybody I know is going to vote for you. (*A pause.*) I was going to put one of your stickers on my taxi but the company said it was against their policy.

PALANTINE: (*Pleasant*) I'll tell you, Travis, I've learned more about this country sitting in taxi-cabs than in the boardroom of General Motors.

TOM: (*Joking*) And in some other places too . . .

(PALANTINE, *his* ASSISTANT *and* TOM *all laugh.*

PALANTINE, *quickly reassuming his canditorial mien, speaks to* TRAVIS.)

PALANTINE: Travis, what single thing would *you* want the next President of this country to do most?

TRAVIS: I don't know, sir. I don't follow political issues much.

PALANTINE: There must be something . . .

TRAVIS: (*Thinks*) Well, he should clean up this city here. It's full of filth and scum; scum, and filth. It's like an open sewer. Sometimes I can hardly take it. Some days I go out and smell it then I get headaches that just stay and never go away. We need a President that would clean up this whole mess. Flush it out.

(PALANTINE *is not a Hubert Humphrey-type professional bullshitter, and* TRAVIS's *intense reply stops him dead in his tracks. He is forced to fall back on a stock answer, but he tries to give it some meaning.*)

PALANTINE: (*After a pause*) I know what you mean, Travis, and it's not going to be easy. We're going to have to make some radical changes.

TRAVIS: (*Turning the wheel*) Damn straight.

(*Travis's taxi pulls up in front of the Barclay Hotel.*

PALANTINE *and* TOM *get out of the cab. The* ASSISTANT *stays in the back seat a moment to pay* TRAVIS.

PALANTINE *looks in front window of cab momentarily and nods goodbye to* TRAVIS.)

PALANTINE: Nice talking to you, Travis.

TRAVIS: (*Calling back*) Thank you, sir. You're a good man, sir. (*Travis's taxi departs.*

PALANTINE *and assistants walk up carpet to the hotel. Close-up of* PALANTINE *as he stops, turns back and watches Travis's departing taxi.*

PALANTINE *turns back and ascends the hotel steps with his assistants.*)

DATE NIGHT

Manhattan street. Early evening.

TRAVIS, *dressed up to the eyeballs, walks brightly down the sidewalk. His face is freshly shaved, his hair combed, his tie straightened.*

He pauses in a store window to check his appearance.

Under his arm he carries the gift-wrapped Kristofferson record album.

Outside Palantine headquarters BETSY, *smartly dressed, waves goodbye to another campaign worker and walks out the door to greet* TRAVIS.

A short while later, TRAVIS *and* BETSY *are walking down Broadway towards Times Square.* BETSY *does not let their bodies touch as they walk although* TRAVIS *contemplates edging closer to her.*

BETSY *has opened the package and is admiring the record – or, rather,* TRAVIS's *sentiment behind giving it.*

TRAVIS *looks round with pride: this is a moment to savour in his life – one of the few.*

BETSY: You didn't have to spend your money –

TRAVIS: (*Interrupting*) Hell, what else can I do with it all?
(BETSY *notices that the seal on the record has not been broken.*)

BETSY: Travis, you haven't even played the record?

TRAVIS: (*Evasive*) Yeah, well my stereo player is broke. But I'm sure the record is OK.

BETSY: Your stereo broke? God, I could hardly stand that. I *live* on music.

29

TRAVIS: I don't follow music much. I'd like to though. (*Second thought*) Honest.

BETSY: (*Pointing to album*) So you haven't heard this record yet?

TRAVIS: No. (*Sly smile*) I thought maybe you could play it for me on your player.

(BETSY's *face backtracks a bit. Maybe she was wrong to go out with this fellow she doesn't know.*

She makes a polite laugh.

Later. TRAVIS *and* BETSY *are in Times Square, turning the corner from Broadway to 42nd Street.* TRAVIS *carries the album under his arm.*

They approach the garish marquee of a large midtown porno theatre advertising The Swedish Marriage Manual. *The box office is flanked on both sides by glass cages filled with explicit publicity stills. Offending portions have been blocked out with black tape.*

TRAVIS *steps over to the window and buys two $5 tickets.*

BETSY, *befuddled, watches him. She doesn't know what to say.*

TRAVIS *returns with the tickets.*

BETSY *still has not fully comprehended what is happening.*)

BETSY: What are you doing?

TRAVIS: (*Innocent*) I bought a couple of tickets.

BETSY: But this is a porno movie.

TRAVIS: No, these are the kind that couples go to. They're not like the other movies. All kinds of couples go. Honest. I've seen them.

(TRAVIS *seems confused. He is so much a part of his own world, he fails to comprehend another's world. Compared to the movies he sees, this is respectable. But then there's also something that* TRAVIS *could not even acknowledge, much less admit: that he really wants to get this pure white girl into that dark porno theatre.*

He makes an awkward gesture to escort BETSY *into the theatre.*

BETSY *looks at the tickets, at the theatre, at* TRAVIS. *She mentally shakes her head and walks toward the turnstile. She thinks to herself: 'What the hell. What can happen?' She's always been curious about these pictures anyway, and – like all women, no matter how intelligent – she's been raised not to offend her date. A perverse logic which applies even more in offsetting circumstances like these.*

30

Inside the theatre. TRAVIS *escorts* BETSY *to an empty centre row.* TRAVIS *was right. Couples do go to films like this. There are at least six or seven other men with their bewigged 'dates'.* TRAVIS *settles into his familiar porno theatre slouch.* BETSY *looks curiously from side to side.*
On screen, a conservatively dressed middle-aged woman is speaking in Swedish about the importance of a healthy sex life in a happy marriage. Subtitles translate her words. Then, without warning, there is a direct cut to a couple copulating on a sterile table-like bed.
TRAVIS *watches intently. The colour, however, is slowly draining from* BETSY*'s cheeks. One thought fills her mind: 'What am I doing here?')*

TRAVIS: (*To himself*) Damn.
BETSY: What's wrong?
TRAVIS: I forgot to get the Coca-Cola.
  (*That does it.* BETSY *just looks at him for a moment, then gets up and starts to leave.* TRAVIS, *confused, hustles after her. He follows her out of the theatre.*)
  (*On the sidewalk* TRAVIS *catches up with her.*)
TRAVIS: Where are you going?
BETSY: I'm leaving.
TRAVIS: What do you mean?
  (BETSY *looks at* TRAVIS, *trying to understand him.*)
BETSY: These are not the kind of movies I go to.
TRAVIS: Well, I don't follow movies too much . . .
BETSY: You mean these are the only kind of movies you go to?
  (*The ticket girl watches expressionlessly from the booth.*)
TRAVIS: This is sort of high class . . .
BETSY: I mean porno movies.
TRAVIS: (*Hesitant*) Well . . . mostly . . .
BETSY: My God!
TRAVIS: We can go to another movie if you like, I don't care. I got money. There's plenty . . .
  (TRAVIS *gestures toward the long row of 42nd Street marquees, but is interrupted by* BETSY.)
BETSY: If you just wanted to fuck, why didn't you just come right out and say it?
  (TRAVIS *is flabbergasted by* BETSY*'s blunt language. His arm*

31

*still gestures toward the marquees, his lips continue to move, but
words do not come out.*

    Unable to respond to BETSY's *question,* TRAVIS *picks up where
he left off.*)

TRAVIS: There's plenty of movies around here. I haven't seen
    any of them, but I'm sure they're good.

BETSY: No, Travis. You're a sweet guy and all that, but I think
    this is it. I'm going home.

TRAVIS: (*Interrupting*) You mean you don't want to go to a
    movie? (*Pause.*) There's plenty of movies around here.

BETSY: No, I don't feel so good. We're just two very different
    kinds of people, that's all.

TRAVIS: (*Puzzled*) Huh?

BETSY: It's very simple. You go your way, I'll go mine. Thanks anyway, Travis.

TRAVIS: But . . . Betsy . . .

BETSY: I'm getting a taxi.
(*She walks to the kerb.*)

TRAVIS: (*Following her.*) But your record?

BETSY: Keep it.

TRAVIS: Can I call you?
(BETSY *looks for a cab.*)
(*Tender*) Please, Betsy, I bought it for *you*.
(BETSY *looks at his sad, sweet face and relents a bit.*)

BETSY: All right, I'll accept the record.
(BETSY *accepts the record, but quickly turns and hails a taxi.*)
Taxi!
(*A taxi quickly pulls up.*
TRAVIS *feebly protests to no one in particular.*)

TRAVIS: But I *got* a taxi.
(BETSY *gives instructions to cab driver, looks briefly back at* TRAVIS, *then straight ahead. Taxi speeds off.*
TRAVIS *looks around helplessly: a cluster of pedestrians on the crowded street has stopped to watch the argument.* TRAVIS *looks back at the woman in the porno theatre box office, who has also been following the argument.*)

PHONE CALLS AND FLOWERS

Inside Travis's apartment.

TRAVIS *is writing at the table. There are some new items on the table: his giant econo-size bottle of vitamins, a giant econo-size bottle of aspirins, a pint of apricot brandy, a partial loaf of cheap white bread.*

On the wall behind the table hang two more items: a gag sign reading 'One of These Days I'm Gonna Get Organezizied' and an orange-and-black bumper sticker for Charles Palantine.

TRAVIS: (*Voice over*) May 8, 1972. My life has taken another turn again. The days move along with regularity . . .
(*Close-up of notebook:* TRAVIS *is no longer sitting at desk. The pencil rests on the open notebook.*
Later that day: TRAVIS *has pulled his straight-backed chair*

around and is watching his small portable TV, which rests on the upright melon crate. A cereal bowl partially filled with milk rests in his lap. TRAVIS *pours a couple of shots of the apricot brandy into the bowl, dips folded chunks of white bread into the mixture, and eats them. He is watching an early evening news programme. There is the sound of the TV in the background.* CHARLES PALANTINE *is being interviewed somewhere on the campaign trail.*)

. . . one day indistinguishable from the next, a long continuous chain, then suddenly – there is a change.

(BETSY *is walking down a midtown street when* TRAVIS *suddenly appears before her. He has been waiting.*

TRAVIS *tries to make conversation but she doesn't listen. She motions for him to go away and keeps on walking.*

TRAVIS, *protesting, follows.*)

(*Inside a building. Day.*

TRAVIS *speaks intensely into a wall pay-phone.*)

I tried to call her several times.

(*We hear* TRAVIS's *voice on the phone:*) You feeling better? You said you didn't feel so good . . .

But after the first call, she would no longer come to the phone.

(TRAVIS *holds the receiver in his hand. The other party has hung up.*)

(*Tracking shot across interior lower wall of Travis's apartment. Against the stark wall there is a row of wilted and dying floral arrangements. Each one of the four or five bouquets is progressively more wilted than the one closer to the door. They have been returned.*)

I also sent flowers with no luck. I should not dwell on such things, but set them behind me. The smell of the flowers only made me sicker. The headaches got worse. I think I've got stomach cancer. I should not complain so. 'You're only as healthy as you feel.'

(*A drama is acted out at Palantine headquarters:* TRAVIS, *groggy and red-eyed from lack of sleep, walks into the campaign headquarters about noon.*

BETSY *is standing near the rear of the office; she ducks from*

sight when she sees TRAVIS *enter.* TRAVIS's *path is cut short by* TOM's *large-framed body. There is no live sound.*)
I realise now how much she is like the others, so cold and distant. Many people are like that. Women for sure. They're like a union.
(TRAVIS *tries to push his way past* TOM *but* TOM *grabs him.* TRAVIS *says something sharply to* TOM *and the two scuffle.* TOM, *by far the taller and stronger, quickly overcomes* TRAVIS, *wrenching his arm behind his back.*
TRAVIS *kicks and protests as* TOM *leads him to the front door. On the sidewalk,* TRAVIS's *efforts quickly subside when* TOM *motions to a nearby policeman.* TRAVIS *quietens down and walks off.*)

THE PUSSY AND THE .44

TRAVIS *is again making his way through the garish urban night. He stops for a passenger on Park Avenue, a middle-aged professorial executive.*
Close-up of TRAVIS: *his face is expressionless. The man makes himself comfortable in the back seat.*
PROFESSORIAL PASSENGER: Jackson Heights.
   (TRAVIS *has no intention of driving out to Jackson Heights and coming back with a fare.*)
TRAVIS: I'm off duty.
PROFESSORIAL PASSENGER: You mean you don't want to go out to Jackson Heights?
TRAVIS: No, I'm off duty.
PROFESSORIAL PASSENGER: Then how come your 'Off Duty' light wasn't on?
   (TRAVIS *switches on the 'Off Duty' light.*)
TRAVIS: It was on. (*Gesturing towards top of taxi.*) It just takes a while to warm up. Like a TV.
   (TRAVIS *doesn't budge.* PROFESSORIAL PASSENGER *curses to himself and gets out of cab.* TRAVIS *takes off.*
   TRAVIS's *eyes dwell on the young hip couples coming out of an East Side movie house.*
   Later that night, TRAVIS *pulls over for a young (mid-twenties) man wearing a leather sports jacket.*
   TRAVIS *eyes his passenger in a rear-view mirror.*)

YOUNG PASSENGER: 417 Central Park West.
> (*Travis's taxi speeds off.*
> *Later, Travis's taxi slows down as it approaches 400 block of Central Park West.*
> TRAVIS *checks apartment numbers.*)
> Just pull over to the kerb a moment.
> (TRAVIS *turns the wheel.*)
> Yeah, that's fine. Just sit here.
> (TRAVIS *waits impassively. The meter ticks away. After a long pause, the* YOUNG PASSENGER *speaks:*)
> Cabbie, ya see that light up there on the seventh floor, three windows from this side of the building?
> (*Camera closes in on 417 Central Park West: tracking up to the seventh floor, it moves three windows to the right.*)

TRAVIS: (*Out of shot*) Yeah.
> (*A young woman wearing a slip crosses in front of the light.*)

YOUNG PASSENGER: (*Out of shot*) Ya see that woman there?

TRAVIS: (*Out of shot*) Yeah.

YOUNG PASSENGER: (*Out of shot*) That's my wife.
> (*Pause.*)

But it ain't my apartment.
(*Pause.*)
A nigger lives there.
(*Pause.*)
She left me two weeks ago. It took me this long to find out where she went.
(*Pause.*)
I'm gonna kill her.
(*Close-up of* TRAVIS's *face: it is devoid of expression.*)
What do you think of that, cabbie?
(*Close-up of* YOUNG PASSENGER's *face: it is gaunt, drained of blood, full of fear and anger.*
TRAVIS *does not respond.*)
Huh? (*Pause.*) What do you think of that, huh?
(TRAVIS *shrugs, gesturing towards meter.*)
I'm gonna kill her with a .44 Magnum pistol.
(*Camera returns to seventh-floor window. Woman is standing in the light.*)
Did you ever see what a .44 can do to a woman's face, cabbie?
(*Pause.*)
Did you ever see what it can do to a woman's pussy, cabbie?
(TRAVIS *says nothing.*)
I'm going to put it right up to her, cabbie. Right in her, cabbie. You must think I'm real sick, huh? A real pervert. Sitting here and talking about a woman's pussy and a .44, huh?
(*Camera closes in on* TRAVIS's *face: he is watching the woman in the seventh-floor window with complete and total absorption. It's the same glazed-over stare we saw in his eyes as he watched the porno movie.*)

THE TRAVELLING SALESMAN

Brooklyn street corner – day.
TRAVIS *stands near the corner wearing his boots, jeans, western shirt and army jacket.*
He pulls his aspirin bottle out of his pocket, shakes three or four into his palm, pops them into his mouth and chews.

An 'Off Duty' taxi pulls up to the kerb. TRAVIS *gets in.*
DOUGH-BOY *leans back from the wheel and greets* TRAVIS *as he enters.*
DOUGH-BOY: Hey Travis. This here's Easy Andy. He's a travelling salesman.
  (*In the back seat, beside* TRAVIS, *sits* ANDY, *an attractive young man of about twenty-nine. He wears a pin-striped suit, white shirt and floral tie. His hair is modishly long.*)
ANDY: Hello, Travis.
  (TRAVIS *nods as the taxi speeds off.*
  DOUGH-BOY *slows down near an economy hotel. Not a flophouse, but not so fancy they care what the guests do in the privacy of their rooms.*)
ANDY: This is fine, Dough-Boy. (*To* TRAVIS.) Pay Dough-Boy here.
  (TRAVIS *pulls a twenty-dollar bill out of his pocket and gives it to* DOUGH-BOY.)
TRAVIS: Twenty bucks?
DOUGH-BOY: (*Takes bill*) Yeah. Hey thanks. That's real nice, Travis.
  (TRAVIS *and* ANDY *get out of the cab and walk towards the hotel.* DOUGH-BOY *pulls away.*
  As they enter the hotel, they pass a junkie, stoned out and spread-eagled across the hood of a derelict old blue Dodge. Inside the hotel, TRAVIS *follows* ANDY *up the worn carpeted stairs and down the hallway.* ANDY *unlocks the door to one of the rooms. The hotel room is barren and clean; there's no sign anyone is staying in it. The fire-escape is appropriately near.* ANDY *locks the door behind them, steps over to the closet, unlocks it and pulls out two grey Samsonite suitcases – the kind you can drive a truck over.*)
ANDY: Dough-Boy probably told you I don't carry any Saturday Night Specials or crap like that. It's all out of State, clean, brand new, top-of-the-line stuff.
  (ANDY *places the suitcases on the white bedspread. The suitcases are equipped with special locks, which he quickly opens. Stacked in grey packing foam are rows and rows of brand-new hand guns.*)
TRAVIS: You got a .44 Magnum?
ANDY: That's an expensive gun.

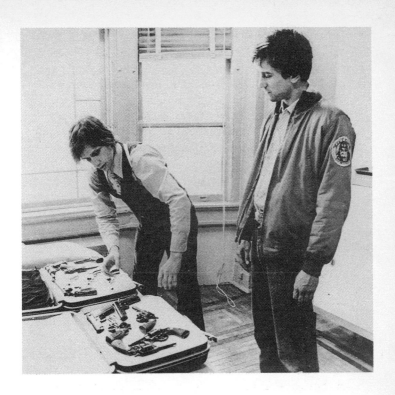

TRAVIS: I got money.

(ANDY *unzips a cowhide leather pouch to reveal a .44 Magnum
pistol. He holds it gingerly, as if it were a precious treasure.*
ANDY *opens the chambers and cradles the long eight-inch barrel
in his palm. The .44 is a huge, oversized, inhuman gun.*)

ANDY: (*Admiringly*) It's a monster. Can stop a car – put a bullet
right into the block. A premium high resale gun. $350 –
that's only a hundred over list.

(EASY ANDY *is a later version of the fast-talking, good-looking
kid in college who was always making money on one scheme or
another. In high school he sold lottery tickets, in college he
scored dope, and now he's hustling hand guns.*
ANDY *holds the Magnum out for* TRAVIS's *inspection. There's
a worshipful close-up of the .44 Magnum. It is a monster.*
TRAVIS *hefts the huge gun. It seems out of place in his hand. It
is built on Michelangelo's scale. The Magnum belongs in the*

39

hand of a marble god, not a slight taxi-driver. TRAVIS *hands the gun back to* ANDY.)
I could sell this gun in Harlem for $500 today – but I just deal high quality goods to high quality people. (*Pause.*) Now this may be a little big for practical use, in which case I'd recommend the .38 Smith and Wesson Special. Fine solid gun – nickel plated. Snub-nosed, otherwise the same as the service revolver. Now that'll stop anything that moves and it's handy, flexible. The Magnum, you know, that's only if you want to splatter it against the wall. The movies have driven up the price of the Magnum anyway. Everybody wants them now. But the Wesson .38 – only $250 – and worth every dime of it. (*He hefts .38.*) Throw in a holster for $10.
(TRAVIS *hefts the nickel-plated .38, points it out the window.*) Some of these guns are like toys, but a Smith and Wesson, man, you can hit somebody over the head with it and it will still come back dead on. Nothing beats quality. (*Pause.*) You interested in an automatic?

TRAVIS: I want a .32. Revolver. And a palm gun. That .22 there.

ANDY: That's the Colt .25 – a fine little gun. Don't do a lotta damage, but it's as fast as the Devil. Handy little gun, you can carry it almost anywhere. I'll throw it in for another $125.
(TRAVIS *holds the .32 revolver, hefts it, slips it under his belt and pulls his shirt over it. He turns from side to side, to see how it rides in his waist.*)

TRAVIS: How much for everything?

ANDY: The .32's $150 – and you're really getting a good deal now – and all together it comes to, ah, seven eighty-five for four pieces and a holster. Hell, I'll give you the holster, we'll make it seven seventy-five and you've got a deal – a good one.

TRAVIS: How much to get a permit to carry?

ANDY: Well, you're talking big money now. I'd say at least five grand, maybe more, and it would take a while to check it out. The way things are going now $5,000 is probably low. You see, I try not to fool with the small-time crap. Too risky, too little bread. Say 6 G's, but if I get the permit it'll be as solid as the Empire State Building.

TRAVIS: Nah, this'll be fine.

ANDY: You can't carry in a cab even with a permit – so why bother?

TRAVIS: Is there a firing range around?

ANDY: Sure, here, take this card. Go to this place and give 'em the card. They'll charge you, but there won't be any hassle.

(TRAVIS *pulls out a roll of crisp one-hundred-dollar bills and counts off eight.*)

You in 'Nam? Can't help but notice your jacket?

TRAVIS: (*Looking up*) Huh?

ANDY: Vietnam? I saw it on your jacket. Where were you? Bet you got to handle a lot of weapons out there.

(TRAVIS *hands* ANDY *the bills.* ANDY *counts them and gives* TRAVIS *a twenty and a five.*)

TRAVIS: Yeah. I was all around. One hospital, then the next.

ANDY: (*As he counts*) It's hell out there all right. A real shit-eatin' war. I'll say this, though: it's bringing back a lot of fantastic guns. The market's flooded. Colt automatics are all over. (*Pockets the money.*)

TRAVIS: (*Intensely*) They'd never get me to go back. They'd have to shoot me first. (*Pause.*) You got anything to carry these in? (*Gestures to pistols.*)

(TRAVIS *is like a light-switch: for long periods he goes along dark and silent, saying nothing; then suddenly, the current is turned on and the air is filled with the electricity of his personality.* TRAVIS's *inner intensity sets* ANDY *back a bit, but he quickly recovers.*)

ANDY: Sure.

(ANDY *pulls a gym bag from under the bed. He wraps the guns in the sheet in the bag and zips it up. An identical gym bag can be partially seen under the bed. He hands* TRAVIS *the bag.*)

You like ball games?

TRAVIS: Huh?

ANDY: I can get you front and centre. What do you like? I can get you Mets, Yankees, Knicks, Rangers? Hell, I can get you the Mayor's box.

TRAVIS: Nah. I ain't interested.

41

(ANDY *closes and locks the suitcases.*)

ANDY: OK, OK.

> (TRAVIS *turns to leave.*)
>
> Wait a second, Travis. I'll walk you out.

TRAVIS GETS ORGANIZED

Several weeks later. The face of Travis's apartment has changed.
The long, blank wall behind the table is now covered with tacked-up
charts, pictures, newspaper clippings, maps. Camera does not come
close enough to discern the exact contents of these clippings.

Close-up of TRAVIS *in the middle of the floor doing push-ups. He is*
bareback, wearing only his jeans. There is a long scar across his left
side.

TRAVIS: (*Voice over*) May 29, 1972. I must get in shape. Too
much sitting has ruined my body. Twenty-five push-ups
each morning, one hundred sit-ups, one hundred knee-
bends. I have quit smoking.

> (TRAVIS *still bareback, passes his stiff arm through the flame of*
> *a gas burner without flinching a muscle.*)

Total organization is necessary. Every muscle must be
tight.

> (*At the firing range. The cracking sound of rapid-fire pistol*
> *shots fills the musty air of the firing range. The walls are*
> *heavily soundproofed, and sawdust is spread over the floor.*
> TRAVIS *stands rock solid, firing the .44 Magnum at an arm's*
> *length. With each blasting discharge from the Magnum,*
> TRAVIS's *body shudders and shakes, his arm rippling back.*
> TRAVIS *quickly bolts himself upright, as if each recoil from the*
> *giant gun was a direct attack on his masculinity.*
> TRAVIS *fires the Magnum as quickly as he can re-set, re-aim*
> *and re-fire. The Magnum empty, he sets it down, picks up the*
> *.38 Special and begins firing as soon as he can aim. After the*
> *.38 comes the .25: it is as if he were in a contest to see how*
> *quickly he can fire the pistols. After all the guns are discharged,*
> *he begins reloading them without a moment's hesitation.*
> *Downrange, the red and white targets have the black outline of*
> *a human figure drawn over them. The contour-man convulses*
> *under the steady barrage of Travis's rapid-fire shots.*)

(*Inside the apartment.* TRAVIS, *now wearing an unfastened green plaid western shirt, sits at the table writing in his diary. The vial of Bennies rests on the table.*)

My body fights me always. It won't work, it won't sleep, it won't shit, it won't eat.

(*Later.* TRAVIS, *his shirt still open revealing his bare chest, sits on his straight-backed chair watching the TV. The .44 Magnum rests on his lap.*

The TV is broadcasting Rock Time, *a late-afternoon local teenage dance and rock show. On screen young teenyboppers are dancing, and the TV cameraman, as any devotee of the genre knows, is relentlessly zooming-in on their firm young breasts, fannies and crotches – a sensibility which reflects* TRAVIS's *own. These supper-hour rock dance shows are the most unabashedly voyeuristic form of broadcasting the medium has yet developed.*

The hard rock number ends, and the TV camera cuts to the local DISC JOCKEY, *a hirsute plastic-looking man of about thirty-five. Five scrumptious teenyboppers are literally hanging on his shoulders and arms, their faces turned up to him in droolish awe. Out of his mouth comes an incessant stream of disc jockey blather. He is the complete asshole.*)

TV DISC JOCKEY: Freshingly, fantastic, freaked-out dance time. Can you dig it? Dig on it. You got it, flaunt it.

(TRAVIS *watches the show, his face hard and unmoving. He is as the Scriptures would say, pondering all these things in his heart. Why is it the assholes get all the beautiful young chicks? He takes a swig of peach brandy.*)

THE $20 RIDE

Early evening, about 6.30 p.m. Travis's taxi, with 'Off Duty' light on, sits near the kerb somewhere in midtown Manhattan.

TRAVIS *runs his hand down the left side of his jacket, attempting to smooth out the bulge in it.*

He opens his jacket partially, checking underneath. There rests the nickel-plated .38 Special in its holster.

From his point of view down the street where Travis's taxi is

44

parked: several blocks ahead the red, white and blue Palantine campaign headquarters are visible.

TRAVIS's *eyes resume their watch.*

TRAVIS *starts the cab and drives towards the Palantine headquarters.*

Tracking point-of-view shot of row of storefronts leading up to Palantine headquarters. Passes headquarters: it is half-empty. A few stalwart supporters continue to work towards the rear of the office. Betsy's desk is vacant.

Sign in window reads: 'ONLY 4 MORE DAYS UNTIL ARRIVAL OF CHARLES PALANTINE.'

Travis's 'Off Duty' light goes off as he speeds up and heads towards a prospective fare.

Later that night, about 9.30. Uptown – 128th and Amsterdam: 'The Jungle'. Travis's taxi pulls up to an address, lets off young black man.

TRAVIS *receives fare and tip, takes off.*

TRAVIS's *point-of-view as he works his way through Harlem back down Seventh Avenue. Cluster of young black street punks pretends to hail cab – we ignore them. One throws wine bottle which crashes in our path – taxi swerves to avoid it.*

Camera tracks through sidewalk crowds with the roving, suspicious, antagonistic eye of a taxi driver.

Later that night, about 12.30. TRAVIS *is on the Lower East Side, somewhere on B Street, east of Tompkins Square.*

The sidewalks are populated with the remains of what was once the hippie movement: teenage street-walkers, junkies, thugs, emaciated loners on the prowl.

Travis's taxi pulls over, letting out a passenger.

TRAVIS *pockets his fare, but the rear right door doesn't slam – instead there is the sound of another person jumping into the cab.*

TRAVIS *checks the back seat in the rear-view mirror: there sits a pale hippie prostitute.*

The girl is, at best, fourteen or fifteen, although she has been made up to look older. She wears floppy, Janis Joplin-style clothes. Her face is pallid. She wears large blue-tinted sunglasses and multi-coloured leg stockings. Her name, as we shall learn later, is IRIS.

TRAVIS *hesitates, looking at her in the mirror.*

IRIS: Come on, Mister, let's get outta here – quick.

    (TRAVIS *moves to activate the meter, when the rear door opens.*

IRIS *is helped out of the cab by a man* TRAVIS *cannot see.*)
SPORT: (*To* IRIS) Come on, baby, let's go. This is all a real
  drag.
  (IRIS *lets herself be taken out of the cab. The rear door closes.*
  SPORT *leans partially in the front window, throwing something*
  on the front seat. TRAVIS *looks: it is a crumpled twenty-dollar*
  bill.)
Just forget all about this, cabbie. It's nothing.
  (TRAVIS *cannot see the* SPORT's *face completely, but notices he*
  is wearing a lime-green jacket. The voice is that of a man in his
  early twenties.
  TRAVIS *turns to catch a glimpse of* SPORT *as he walks off with*
  IRIS.
  TRAVIS *shrugs and turns around. His taxi pulls away.*)

FOREPLAY TO GUNPLAY

Early morning, 6.00 a.m. Quitting-time – TRAVIS *pulls into taxi*
garage.
TRAVIS *pulls into his stall.*
He sits in driver's seat, thinking a moment. He looks to his right: the
crumpled twenty-dollar bill still lies there, untouched since it was
thrown there six hours previously.
TRAVIS *reluctantly picks it up and stuffs it into his jacket pocket as*
he gets out of the cab. He gathers up his time report and heads
towards book-in table.
A short while later, TRAVIS *is walking down the sidewalk near the*
taxi garage. His hands are in his jacket pockets, obscuring the slight
bulge on his left side.
He turns into the box office of the porno theatre. He reaches into
jacket pocket for money to purchase ticket and pulls out crumpled
twenty-dollar bill. He decides not to use it, and pays for ticket out of
his wallet instead.
TRAVIS *walks past the concession stand* en route *to the darkened*
theatre auditorium. A young man is now sitting listlessly behind the
concessions counter.
Inside the porno theatre auditorium TRAVIS *slouches down into his*
seat, his face glowing in the reflected light from the screen.
FEMALE MOVIE VOICE: (*Out of shot*) Oh, come on, now, down,

46

lick it, come on . . . Mmm, that's good. Ahh, ahh,
more . . .
(TRAVIS *averts his eyes as the action on screen becomes too*
graphic. Placing his stiffened right hand beside his eyes,
TRAVIS *can, by turning it inward, shut off or open up his field*
of vision by small degrees.
MOVIE VOICE *diminishes, replaced by sound of* TRAVIS's *voice*
over.)
TRAVIS: (*Voice over*) The idea has been growing in my brain . . .
(*Tracking shot to wall of Travis's apartment. Camera moves*
slowly across wall covered with clippings, notes, maps, pictures.
We now see their contents clearly:
The wall is covered with Charles Palantine political
paraphernalia; there are pictures of him, newspaper articles,
leaflets, bumper stickers. As the camera moves along it discovers
a sketch of Plaza Hotel, Kennedy Airport and cut-up sections
of city maps with notations written in. There is a lengthy New
York Times *clipping detailing the increased Secret Security*
Protection during the primaries. A section pertaining to
PALANTINE *is underlined. Further along there is a sheet*
reading 'traveling schedule' and a calendar for June with finely
written notations written over the dates.)
. . . for some time. True Force. All the king's men cannot
put it back together again.
(*As the camera reaches the end of its track, it finds* TRAVIS,
standing, his shirt open, by the mattress. He is wearing the
empty holster, and the .44 is in his hand.
In the shots that follow TRAVIS *gives the audience a lesson in*
gunmanship:
TRAVIS *practises fast-drawing the .38 Special from his holster*
and firing it.
He hooks the .44 into his pants behind his back and practises
withdrawing it. He holds the .44 firmly at an arm's length,
tightening his forearm muscles.
He has worked out a system of metal gliders taped to his inner
forearm, whereby the Colt .25 can rest hidden behind the upper
forearm until a spring near the elbow is activated, sending the
.25 flying down the gliders into his palm. He has cut open his
shirt to accommodate the gun mechanism and now checks in the
mirror to see how well the gun is hidden.

47

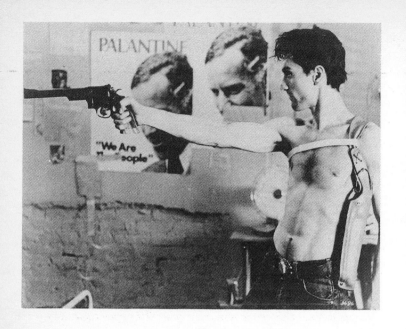

*He straps an Army combat knife to his calf and cuts a slit in his
jeans where the knife can be pulled out quickly.*
*He now tries on various combinations of shirts, sweaters and
jackets in front of the mirror to see how well he can hide all the
handguns he wishes to carry. Finally, wearing two western
shirts, a sweater and jacket, he manages to obscure the location
of all three guns, although he resembles a hunter bundled up
against the Arctic winter.*
*He sits at the table dum-dumming the .44 bullets – cutting 'x's'
across the bullet heads.*
*From his point of view he scans the objects of his room through
the scope of the .38.*
TRAVIS *stands in the middle of his apartment, staring at his
Palantine wall. His eyes are glazed with introspection; he sees
nothing but himself.)*
Listen, you screwheads:
Here is a man . . .
(TRAVIS *lies on his mattress, all bundled up in his shirts,
sweater, jacket and guns. His face is turned towards the ceiling,
but his eyes are closed. Although the room is flooded with light,*

*he is finally catching some sleep. The big furry animal drifts
into his own world.*)
. . . who wouldn't take it any more, a man who stood up
against the scum, the cunts, the dogs, the filth. Here is . . .
(*Voice trails off.*
*Close-up of diary: entry ends 'Here is' followed by erratic series
of dots.*)

INCIDENT IN A DELI

Night: the taxis are roaming the slick streets.
Sometimes, after 2.00 a.m., TRAVIS *pulls his cab to the kerb near
an all-night delicatessen in Spanish Harlem. The streets are
relatively deserted.*
TRAVIS *waves to storekeeper as he walks past counter.*
TRAVIS: Hey Melio.
   (*Spanish rhythm-and-blues blares from a cheap radio.*
   TRAVIS *walks over to dairy counter in rear of the store, picks
   out a pint of chocolate milk, goes over to the open cooler and
   picks through various chilled prepackaged sandwiches. He
   overhears a voice as he looks at the sandwiches.*
   When TRAVIS *returns to the counter with the chocolate milk
   and a sandwich in one hand, he sees a young black man
   holding a gun on* MELIO. *The* STICK-UP MAN *is nervous,
   hopped-up, or both: he bounces on the balls of his cheap, worn
   black tennis shoes – a strung-out junkie on a desperation ride.*
   The STICK-UP-MAN, *a thorough unprofessional, doesn't notice*
   TRAVIS.
   MELIO *watches the* STICK-UP MAN *closely, deciding what to
   do himself.*)
STICK-UP MAN: (*Shaking gun*) Come on, man. Quick, quick,
quick – let's see that bread.
   (*It doesn't take* TRAVIS *long to decide what to do: without
   hesitation he pulls his .32 from his jacket pocket.*)
TRAVIS: Hey dude!
   (STICK-UP MAN, *surprised, turns towards* TRAVIS, *finding
   only an exploding .32. The* STICK-UP MAN'*s lower jaw bursts
   open with blood as he reels and crashes to the floor. There is no
   emotion on* TRAVIS'*s face.*
   As the STICK-UP MAN *falls,* MELIO *leans over the counter,*

49

*wielding his battered .38. He is about to fire when he realizes
he is already dead.*

MELIO, *charged up, turns his gun towards* TRAVIS, *then,
realizing the danger is over, lowers it again.*)

MELIO: Thanks, man. Figured I'd get him on the way out.

(TRAVIS *sets his .32 on the counter.*)

TRAVIS: You're gonna have to cover me on this one, Melio. I
can't stay for the cop show.

MELIO: You can't do that, Travis. You're my witness.

TRAVIS: The hell I can't. It's no sweat for you. What is this for
you, number five?

(MELIO *smiles and holds up four fingers.*)

MELIO: No, only four. (*Shrugs.*) All right, Travis, I'll do what I
can.

TRAVIS: Thanks a lot.

(TRAVIS *exits.* MELIO *picks up the phone and starts dialling.
The bloody body lies on the floor unmoving.*

TRAVIS, *still carrying his pint of chocolate milk and sandwich,
walks down the empty sidewalk and enters his cab. The street is
deserted.*)

*Direct cut to pornographic movie: this is the first time we have
actually seen the porno movie itself. Several actors and actresses are
dallying on screen in whatever manner the ratings board deems
permissible.*

*Whatever the action, the movie's decor is strictly Zody's – ersatz
landscape paintings, tufted bedspreads. As in most porno films, the
actors look up occasionally towards the camera to receive
instructions. Studio grunts, groans and moans of pleasure have been
dubbed in.*

*Action on screen begins to go into slow motion, the actors and
actresses gradually transforming obscenity into poetry.*

Cut to TRAVIS, *sitting in his chair in his apartment, watching
afternoon soap opera. He is cleaning his .38 and eating from a jar of
apple sauce. Soap opera audio continues.*

He watches the soap opera without expression.

*Sound track of film also slows down, gradually mixing with and
then becoming the sound track of a mid-afternoon TV soap opera.*

*A young girl and boy are talking in those familiar soap-opera voices
about a third party, the girl's mother, who had tried to terminate
their 'relationship'.*

*Cut to television: The boy is visiting the girl in her hospital room.
Both look as if they've stepped out of the Blue Chip Stamp
catalogue.*

SOAP OPERA BOY: Is it that she just doesn't – like me?

SOAP OPERA GIRL: (*Hesitantly*) Well, Jim, it's just that – I don't
    know how to say this – it's that she thinks your parents
    aren't . . . good enough, I guess.

    (TRAVIS, *through cleaning his gun, begins to play a game with
    the television set.*

    *He places the heel of his boot at the top of the melon crate
    which supports the TV. Then, slowly rocking his heel back and
    forth, he sees how far he can tip the melon crate without
    knocking it over.*

    *The TV, still broadcasting the hospital room melodrama, rocks
    back and forth.*

    TRAVIS *pushes the TV further and further until finally the
    inevitable happens – the crate tips backwards, sending the
    portable TV crashing to the floor.*

There is a short flash and the TV screen turns white.
TRAVIS, *realizing what he has done, bends over, turns the TV upright on the floor, fiddles with the knobs, slaps it, and tries to reactivate the vanished image.* TRAVIS's *efforts are futile; a tube has broken, and the TV will not come back to life.*)
TRAVIS: (*To himself*) Damn, damn.
(TRAVIS *bends over in the chair and places his head in his hands, despairing of himself.*)

THE WIZARD SPEAKS

At about 1 a.m. TRAVIS *pulls his cab behind a line of empty taxis parked outside the Bellmore Cafeteria, a cabbie hangout on Park Avenue South.*
He locks his cab and walks past the line of taxis. He sidesteps past two drunken fighting bums and enters the Bellmore.
A loud buzzer rings as TRAVIS *steps into the Bellmore. He pulls a ticket from the dispenser (silencing the buzzer) and walks towards the wall-length counter. An assortment of cabbies are seated around a formica-topped table near the rear of the cafeteria. Some are barely awake, some are eating, the rest are swapping stories and small talk.*
WIZARD, DOUGH-BOY, CHARLIE T *and a* FOURTH CABBIE *are seated at a long table.*
WIZARD: You know Eddie, he's the new hippie kid in our group, long hair . . .
(WIZARD *demonstrates length of hair and others nod.*)
WIZARD: . . . he called up the Dispatcher last night. Charlie McCall, our dispatcher . . .
DOUGH-BOY: One-Ball McCall?
WIZARD: That's the guy. Eddie calls him up and says, 'Hey, what do you want me to do? I'm over here at Poly Prep. I got a girl in the back and she doesn't have the fare. She wants me to come in back and collect. What should I do?'
(*The cabbies laugh. Across the cafeteria* TRAVIS *selects a cup of coffee and some pastries.*)
CHARLIE T: This is on the two-way with about a hundred and fifty cats listenin' in.
WIZARD: McCall says, 'How much on the meter?' Eddie comes back and says, 'Two-fifty.' McCall says, 'Is she worth it?'
(*More laughter.*)

DOUGH-BOY: Fuckin' One-Ball.

WIZARD: And the kid says, 'Yeah. She's about nineteen, good-lookin'.' McCall says, 'What can I tell you?'

FOURTH CABBIE: Should have told him to get an OK from the front office.

WIZARD: McCall says, 'Well, if you want some help I'll see if I can send some units out.'

CHARLIE T: Yeah. About a hundred and fifty.

DOUGH-BOY: I hope he had a checker.

WIZARD: She was just a kid. Stoned, you know.

(TRAVIS, *carrying his coffee and pastries, walks over to their table.* CHARLIE T *spots him.*)

CHARLIE T: Hiya Killer.

(CHARLIE *forms his hand into a pistol, cocks and fires, making the sound 'Pgghew'.* TRAVIS *nods.*)

WIZARD: You're getting a rep, Travis.

(TRAVIS *sits down and the other cabbies resume their conversation.*)

CHARLIE T: Got the five you owe me, Killer?

(TRAVIS *reaches into his pocket and pulls out a roll of small denomination bills. The crumpled $20 bill falls on to the table.* TRAVIS *stares at it a moment. He unfolds a five, gives it to* CHARLIE T, *then picks up the crumpled $20 and puts it back into his jacket pocket.*)

WIZARD: (*Out of shot, to* TRAVIS) What's the action around?

TRAVIS: Slow.

CHARLIE T: Shit yes. Night would'a been dead if I hadn't grabbed an outa'towner at Kennedy. Took him round the horn and got a five dollar tip to boot.

WIZARD: (*Joking*) One of these days we're gonna turn you in, Charlie T. Fleecin' the hicks like that.

DOUGH-BOY: Remember the time this cat picks up four dudes from the other side, Pakistanis I think they were, holds up their passports to the toll booth collector on the bridge and charges 'em ten bucks each for 'crossing the border?

(*They all laugh.*)

CHARLIE T: Hell, I know'd you to do worse.

DOUGH-BOY: Least I'm no airport rat. I work the whole town.

CHARLIE T: (*Chuckling*) It's a living.

(WIZARD *gets up to leave.*)

WIZARD: Well, I'm shovin' on.
> (*He nods and walks towards the cashier. After a second's thought,* TRAVIS *calls to him:*)

TRAVIS: Hey Wiz, just a second. I wanna talk to you.
> (WIZARD *waits for* TRAVIS *as he takes a final gulp of coffee and catches up with him.* CHARLIE T *calls to* TRAVIS *as they go:*)

CHARLIE T: See ya, Killer. Don't forget your pea shooter.
> (CHARLIE T *cocks his imaginary gun again, fires and chuckles.* WIZARD *and* TRAVIS *nod goodbye, pay the cashier and exit.* TRAVIS *follows* WIZARD *out on to the sidewalk.* TRAVIS *follows* WIZARD *as he walks towards his cab. He has something on his mind, something he wants to talk to* WIZARD *about.*)

TRAVIS: (*As they walk*) Hey Wiz.

WIZARD: Yeah?
> (WIZARD *leans back against his cab.* TRAVIS *is about to speak when he spots a group of black and Puerto Rican street punks, aged between twelve and fifteen, jiving down the sidewalk towards him. One tosses a spray-paint can around his back, basketball style. Another mocks as if he's going to scratch a key along one of the cabs.*
> WIZARD *has no visible reaction. A flash of controlled anger crosses* TRAVIS's *face. He stares at the boy with the poised key. It is the same look that crossed his face in the Harlem Deli. We are reminded with a jolt that the killer lies just beneath* TRAVIS's *surface.*
> *The black punk must instinctively realize this too, because he makes a cocky show of putting the key back into his pocket and be-bopping around* TRAVIS *and* WIZARD.
> *The young mean-streeters continue down the street and* TRAVIS *turns back to* WIZARD.
> *Across the street, in the background, a junkie huddles in a doorway.*)

TRAVIS: (*Hesitant*) Wiz?

WIZARD: Yeah?

TRAVIS: Look ah, we never talked much, you and me . . .

WIZARD: Yeah?

TRAVIS: I wanted to ask you something, on account you've been around so long.

WIZARD: Shoot. They don't call me the Wizard for nothing.

TRAVIS: Well, I just, you know . . .

WIZARD: Things got ya down?

TRAVIS: Real down.

WIZARD: It happens.

TRAVIS: Sometimes it gets so I just don't know what I'm gonna do. I get some real crazy ideas, you know? Just go out and do somethin'.

WIZARD: The taxi life, you mean.

TRAVIS: Yeah.

WIZARD: (*Nods*) I know.

TRAVIS: Like do *anything*, you know.

WIZARD: Travis, look, I dig it. Let me explain. You choose a certain way of life. You live it. It becomes what you are. I've been a hack twenty-seven years, the last ten at night. Still don't own my own cab. I guess that's the way I want it. You see, that must be what I am.

(*A police car stops across the street. Two patrolmen get out and roust the junkie from his doorway.*)
Look, a person does a certain thing and that's all there is to it. It becomes what he is. Why fight it? What do you know? How long you been a hack, a couple months? You're like a peg and you get dropped into a slot and you got to squirm and wiggle around a while until you fit in.

TRAVIS: (*Pause*) That's just about the dumbest thing I ever heard, Wizard.

WIZARD: What do you expect, Bertrand Russell? I've been a cabbie all my life, what do I know? (*Pauses.*) I don't even know what you're talking about.

TRAVIS: Neither do I, I guess.

WIZARD: You fit in. It's lonely, it's rough at first. But you fit in. You got no choice.

TRAVIS: Yeah. Sorry, Wizard?

WIZARD: Don't worry, Killer. You'll be all right. (*Pauses.*) I seen enough to know.

TRAVIS: Thanks.

(WIZARD *gives* TRAVIS *a short wave implying, 'chin up, old boy', and walks around to the driver's side of his cab. He drives off, leaving the street to its natural inhabitants.*)

A NEW FACE IN THE CROWD

Outside, at the Charles Palantine Rally. Day.
A rally platform in a supermarket parking lot somewhere in Queens is draped in red, white and blue bunting.
A crowd of about five hundred strong mills about, waiting for the rally to begin. Piped pop-country music plays over the loudspeaker system.
A cadre of secret service men, with their distinctive metallic grey suits, sun glasses and football physiques, stands out in the crowd.
On the platform are seated an assortment of local politicos as well as some Palantine workers and advisers.
TOM *is silently reading something of the podium, and* BETSY *stands on the platform steps talking to another worker.*
TOM *looks up and to his left for a moment, then returns to what he was reading. Then he returns his gaze to the upper left, watching something very closely.*
After a moment he walks over to the steps where BETSY *is standing.*

TOM: Betsy, come over here a moment.

BETSY: What is it? I'm busy.

TOM: (*Insistent*) Just follow me.

(BETSY *excuses herself and walks across the platform with* TOM. *As they stand to the rear of the platform,* TOM *secretively makes a gesture with his eyes and says out of the side of his mouth.*)

TOM: Look there.

(*Her eyes follow his.*)

No, over further – get your glasses – yes, over there. Isn't that little guy the same guy that was bugging you around the office about a month ago?

(BETSY, *putting on her glasses, looks closely. She tries not to make her stare too obvious.*)

BETSY: No, I don't think so.

(*A pause.*)

That's someone else.

TOM: Now look more closely. Look around the eyes and chin. See? See there?

(*Camera closes in on* TRAVIS *standing in the crowd: he has shaved his head to a short stubble. There he is: brush-cut, wearing a giant grin and a large 'Palantine '72' button. Although it is a pleasant sunny day,* TRAVIS *is wearing a bulky bulged-out Army jacket.*

TRAVIS *looks warily from side to side and vanishes in the crowd.*)

(*A short while later,* TRAVIS *walks up to a* SECRET SERVICE MAN *standing near the fringes of the crowd. The* SECRET SERVICE MAN – *in sun glasses, grey suit, ever-roving eyes – is immediately indentifiable.*

Whenever TRAVIS *confronts a symbol of authority, he becomes like a young boy. This time is no exception, although one suspects there is a plan hatching beneath the boyish exterior. The* SECRET SERVICE MAN, *for his part, is about as talkative as the Sphinx.*)

TRAVIS: Are you a Secret Service Man?

SECRET SERVICE MAN: (*Indifferently*) Why do you ask?

TRAVIS: I've seen a lot of suspicious-looking people around here today.

(SECRET SERVICE MAN *glances at* TRAVIS *momentarily.*)

SECRET SERVICE MAN: Who?

TRAVIS: Oh, lots. I don't know where they all are now. There used to be one standing over there. (*Points.*)

(SECRET SERVICE MAN's *gaze follows* TRAVIS's *finger for a second, then returns to* TRAVIS.)

Is it hard to get to be a Secret Service Man?

SECRET SERVICE MAN: Why?

TRAVIS: I kinda' thought I might make a good one. I'm very observant.

SECRET SERVICE MAN: Oh?

TRAVIS: I was in the Army too. (*A pause.*) And I'm good with crowds.

(*The* SECRET SERVICE MAN *is starting to get interested in* TRAVIS: *he definitely ranks as a suspicious character.*)

SECRET SERVICE MAN: Is that so?

TRAVIS: What kind of guns do you guys use? .38s?

(*The* SECRET SERVICE MAN *decides it's time to get some more information on* TRAVIS:)

SECRET SERVICE MAN: Look, um, if you give me your name and address, we'll send you the information on how to apply.

TRAVIS: You would, huh?

SECRET SERVICE MAN: (*Taking out notepad*) Sure.

TRAVIS: My name is Henry Krinkle – that's with a K. K-R-I-N-K-L-E. I live at 13 1/2 Hopper Avenue, Fair Lawn, New Jersey. Zip code 07410. (*A pause.*) Got that?

SECRET SERVICE MAN: Sure, Henry. I got it all. We'll send you all the stuff all right.

TRAVIS: Great, hey. Thanks a lot.

(*The* SECRET SERVICE MAN *motions to a secret service photographer to catch a picture of* TRAVIS. TRAVIS *notices this, and quickly slips away into the crowd.*)

(TRAVIS *sits at his desk in his apartment, writing. He wears jeans, western shirt and empty holster.*)

TRAVIS: (*Voice over*) June 11. Eight rallies in six more days. The time is coming.

Night. Travis's taxi picks up a fare in the midtown area and heads downtown.

Lower East Side. TRAVIS *lets off fare on B Street and cuts across towards Tompkins Square.*

TRAVIS *turns the corner when* skreetch! *he suddenly hits the brakes, causing the cab to rock back and forth.*

He has almost hit a young girl recklessly crossing the street. She thumps her hand on the taxi hood to regain her balance and stares in shock through the front window. Close-up of girl's face.

TRAVIS *recognizes her face: it's* IRIS, *the girl in his taxi a week or so before.* IRIS *looks at* TRAVIS *sharply then turns and continues walking.*

TRAVIS'*s eyes follow her and she rejoins a girlfriend. They are both dressed as hippie hookers: sloppy clothes, boots, jeans, floppy hats. And the old come-hither walk is ummistakable.*

TRAVIS *follows* IRIS *and her girlfriend slowly as they walk down the sidewalk.*

TRAVIS'*s point of view: He examines them from bottom to top – boots, legs, thighs, breasts, faces, hats.*

As TRAVIS *rolls astride the girls, he notices the familiar fringe of a suede jacket standing in the shadows. The girls look towards the shadowed figure, smile, acknowledge some unheard comment, and continue on.*

IRIS *looks back uneasily at Travis's taxi and continues on.*

On the corner stand two well-to-do college students, somewhat out of place in this environment, but making every attempt to groove on it. They are high on something or other.

The girls spot the college students and walk over to them. They exchange some small talk and walk off together. There is little subtlety involved: it is obviously a pick-up.

TRAVIS *must negotiate a turn around the corner if he is to continue following the girls and their collegiate johns. This is not so easy, since the traffic is heavy.*

As TRAVIS *slows down to make the turn, he notices another hippie hooker who had been watching him watching* IRIS *and her girlfriend. She walks over to the taxi, leans in the open left front window and gives* TRAVIS *the come-on disguised as an innocent question:*

HIPPIE HOOKER: (*Close-up*) Hey, cabbie! You comin' or goin'? (TRAVIS *quickly turns his face away from her in a combination of shock, embarrassment and revulsion. He is the child caught with his hand in the cookie jar. The very presence of this crassly, openly sexual human being frightens and sickens him. He takes off with a screech. His taxi shoots down the block.*)

CAMPAIGN PROMISES

A hot June day. Travis's taxi, the 'Off Duty' sign on, is parked against the kerb somewhere in Harlem. White cops, secret service men and reporters punctuate the otherwise black crowds walking to and fro in the background.

CHARLES PALANTINE's *voice can be heard coming from a distant loudspeaker system. It is a political rally.*

TRAVIS *sits behind the wheel, coldly staring at something in the distance. His hair, of course, is still clipped short and he wears mirror-reflecting sunglasses. Even though a drop of sweat is working its way down his cheek,* TRAVIS *wears his Army jacket with the bulge on the left side – the .38 Smith and Wesson bulge.*

A block away, PALANTINE *stands on a platform outside his uptown campaign headquarters. On the platform sit an array of black dignitaries. Near by we recognize the* SECRET SERVICE MAN *who* TRAVIS *spoke to at the earlier rally: he scans the crowd anxiously.*

PALANTINE *is speaking animatedly. He is an excellent speaker and captures the attention. He drives hard towards his arguments, crashes down on his points. His strained voice rings with sincerity and anger. Close-up of* PALANTINE *as he speaks. He is dressed in rolled-up shirtsleeves and sweat pours down his face.*

PALANTINE: The time has come to put an end to the things that divide us: racism, poverty, war – and to those persons who seek to divide us. Never have I seen such a group of high officials from the President to Senate leaders to Cabinet members . . .

(*Cut to* TRAVIS: *no expression.* PALANTINE's *words are barely distinguishable from a block away.*)

(*In distance.*)

. . . pit black against white, young against old, sew anger, disunity and suspicion – and all in the name of the 'good of the country'. Well, their game is over. (*Applause.*) All their names are over. Now is the time to stand up against such foolishness, propaganda and demagoguery. Now is the time for one man to stand up and accept his neighbour, for one man to give in order that all might receive. Is unity and love of common good such a lost thing?

(*All live sound ceases as* TRAVIS's *narration begins. He is reading from a letter or card he has just written.*
As he speaks we see shots of PALANTINE *speaking, a seated row of young black Palantine red, white and blue bedecked cheerleaders, secret service agents, examining the crowd and so forth. These shots have no direct relationship to the narration.*)

TRAVIS: (*Voice over, reading*)

'Dear Father and Mother,

June is the month, I remember, which brings not only your wedding anniversary, but also Father's Day and Mother's birthday. I'm sorry I can't remember the exact dates, but I hope this card will take care of all of them.

I'm sorry I again cannot send you my address like I promised to last year, but the sensitive nature of my work for the Army demands utmost secrecy. I know you will understand.

I am healthy and well and making lots of money. I have been going with a girl for several months and I know you would be proud if you could see her. Her name is Betsy, but I can tell you no more than that – '

(*As* TRAVIS *reads third paragraph, a* POLICEMAN *is seen walking from behind Travis's taxi to his window.*
The POLICEMAN's *voice comes during a pause in the narration. Live sound resumes.*)

POLICEMAN: (*Standing near window*) Hey, cabbie, you can't park here.

TRAVIS: (*Penitent*) Sorry, officer.

POLICEMAN: You waiting for a fare?

(POLICEMAN *leans his head in window, inspecting the cab. As he does,* TRAVIS *slides his right hand into the left side of his jacket, ready to draw his revolver.*)

TRAVIS: No, officer.

POLICEMAN: All right, move it.
> (TRAVIS *starts up his taxi and drives off.*
> *Live sound again ceases as* TRAVIS *resumes reading letter as taxi drives away.*
> *As* TRAVIS *reads final paragraph, scene cuts to inside his apartment where* TRAVIS *sits at his table.*)

TRAVIS: (*Voice over, resuming reading*)
> 'I hope this card finds you all well, as it does me. I hope no one has died. Don't worry about me. One day there will be a knock on the door and it will be me.

> Love, Travis.'

> (TRAVIS, *at his desk, examines the card upon which he has just written this letter.*
> *Close-up cover of card. It is a 25¢ wedding anniversary card with a four-colour embossed cover. The design could only be described as kitsch. A cartoon Mr and Mrs All-America stand before an outdoor barbecuing grill, clicking salt and pepper shakers in a toast. Sentiment reads:*

> HAPPY ANNIVERSARY
> *To a Couple*
> *Who Have Found*
> *the Perfect Combination*
> *For Marriage . . .*

> *The card opens to read:*
> LOVE!
> *Underneath the word 'Love!' begins Travis's short message to his parents, a message which extends to the back cover of the card.*)

SWEET IRIS

Night on the Lower East Side. TRAVIS *sits parked in the dark shadows of a side street. The lone wolf waits.*

TRAVIS *watches the slum goddesses as they work the section of the street reserved for hippie hookers.*

TRAVIS's *point of view: some of the young street girls are arrogant, almost aggressive, others are more insecure and inexperienced.*

A black man charges down the sidewalk across the street from

TRAVIS. *He walks at a fast, maniacal clip, looking only at the sidewalk in front of him. Out of his mouth comes a continuous stream of invective: 'That-cock-sucking-crazy-no-good-asshole-bitch-when-I-get-my-fucking-fingers-on-her-nigger-tits-I'm-gonna-ring-em-and-shit-up-her ass . . .' and so on. He is out of control. Nobody seems to notice or care.*

TRAVIS *takes a swig of peach brandy and continues his stake-out. Finally,* TRAVIS *spies the object of his search:* IRIS *walks down the sidewalk with her girlfriend.* IRIS *wears her large blue sunglasses.* TRAVIS *checks to see if his .38 is in place (it is), opens the door and exits from the cab.*

Flipping up the collar of his Army jacket, TRAVIS *slouches over and walks towards* IRIS. *He sidles up next to her and walks beside her:* TRAVIS *always looks most suspicious when he's trying to appear innocent.*

TRAVIS: (*Shy*) Hello.

IRIS: You looking for some action?

TRAVIS: Well . . . I guess so.

IRIS: (*Eyeing him*) All right. (*A pause.*) You see that guy over there? (*Nods.*) His name is Sport. Go talk to him. I'll wait here.

> (TRAVIS's *eyes follow* IRIS's *nod until they reach* SPORT, *standing in a doorway in his lime-green jacket.* TRAVIS *walks towards him.*
>
> SPORT, *a thirtyish white greaser, has the affectations of a black pimp. His hips are jiving, his fingers softly snapping. He sings to himself, 'Going to the chapel, gonna get married . . .' His complexion is sallow; his eyes cold and venal. He could only seem romantic to a confused under-aged runaway.*)

TRAVIS: Your name Sport?

> (SPORT *immediately takes* TRAVIS *for an undercover cop. He extends his crossed wrists as if to be handcuffed.*)

SPORT: Here, officer, take me in. I'm clean. I didn't do it. Got a ticket once in Jersey, that's all. Honest, officer.

TRAVIS: Your name Sport?

SPORT: Anything you say, officer.

TRAVIS: I'm no cop. (*Looks back at* IRIS.) I want some action.

SPORT: I saw. $20 fifteen minutes. $30 half hour.

TRAVIS: Shit.

SPORT: Take it or leave it.

TRAVIS: I'll take it.
    (TRAVIS *digs in his pocket for money.*)
SPORT: No, not me. There'll be an elderly gent to take the
    bread.
    (TRAVIS *turns to walk away.*)
    Catch you later, Copper.
    (TRAVIS *freezes, not saying anything. He turns back towards*
    SPORT.)
TRAVIS: I'm no cop.
SPORT: Well, if you are, it's entrapment already.
TRAVIS: I'm hip.
SPORT: Funny, you don't look hip. (*Laughs.*)
    (TRAVIS *walks back to* IRIS. *She motions for* TRAVIS *to follow*
    her and he does. They turn the corner and walk about a block,
    saying nothing, IRIS *turns into a darkened doorway and*
    TRAVIS *follows her.*
    At the top of the dark stairs IRIS *and* TRAVIS *enter a dimly lit*
    hallway. On either side are doors with apartment numbers.
    IRIS *turns towards the first door, No. 2.*)
IRIS: This is my room.

(*At the far end of the darkened corridor sits a huge* OLD MAN. *His face is obscured by shadow.* TRAVIS *is about to enter the room when the* OLD MAN *speaks up:*)

OLD MAN: Hey cowboy!

(TRAVIS *turns his head towards the* OLD MAN, *who has stood up and is advancing towards him.*)

(*Motioning to Travis's jacket*) The rod. (*A pause.*) Gimme the rod, cowboy.

(TRAVIS *hesitates a moment, uncertain what to do. The* OLD MAN *reaches in Travis's jacket and pulls out the .38 Special.*) This ain't Dodge City, cowboy. You don't need no piece. (*Glances at watch.*) I'm keepin' time.

(TRAVIS *enters No. 2 with* IRIS.

TRAVIS *looks around* IRIS's *room: although dimly lit, the room is brightly decorated. There is an orange shag carpet, deep brown walls and an old red velvet sofa. On the walls are posters of Mick Jagger, Bob Dylan and Peter Fonda. A Neil Young album is playing on a small phonograph.*

This is where IRIS *lives: it bears the individual touch of a young girl.*

IRIS *lights a cigarette, takes a single puff and places it in an ashtray on the bedstand.*)

TRAVIS: Why you hang around with them greasers?

IRIS: A girl needs protection.

TRAVIS: Yeah. From the likes of them.

IRIS: (*Shrugs*) It's your time, mister. Fifteen minutes ain't long. (*Gestures to cigarette.*) That cigarette burns out, your time is up.

(IRIS *sits on the edge of the bed and removes her hat and coat. She takes off her blue-tinted sunglasses – her last defence. Without the paraphernalia of adulthood,* IRIS *looks like the little girl she is. About fourteen, fifteen.*)

TRAVIS: What's your name?

IRIS: Easy.

TRAVIS: That ain't much of a name.

IRIS: It's easy to remember. Easy Lay.

TRAVIS: What's your real name?

IRIS: I don't like my real name.

TRAVIS: (*Insistent*) What's your real name?

IRIS: Iris.

TRAVIS: That's a nice name.

IRIS: That's what you think.

(IRIS *unbuttons her shirt, revealing her small pathetic breasts –*
two young doves hiding from a winter wind. TRAVIS *is*
unnerved by her partial nudity.)

TRAVIS: Don't you remember me? Button your shirt.

(IRIS *buttons only the bottom button on her shirt.*)

IRIS: (*Examining him*) Why? Who are you?

TRAVIS: I drive a taxi. You tried to get away one night.
Remember?

IRIS: No.

TRAVIS: You tried to run away in my taxi but your friend –
Sport – wouldn't let you.

IRIS: I don't remember.

TRAVIS: It don't matter. I'm gonna get you outa' here. (*Looks*
towards door.)

IRIS: We better make it, or Sport'll get mad. How do you want
to make it?

TRAVIS: (*Pressured*) I don't want to make it. I came here to get
you out.

IRIS: You want to make it like this? (*Goes for his fly.*)

(TRAVIS *pushes her hand away. He sits beside her on the edge*
of the bed.)

TRAVIS: (*Taking her by the shoulders*) Can't you listen to me?
Don't you want to get out of here?

IRIS: Why should I want to get out of here? This is where I live.

TRAVIS: (*Exasperated*) But *you're* the one that wanted to get
away. *You're* the one that came into my cab.

IRIS: I must'a been stoned.

TRAVIS: Do they drug you?

IRIS: (*Reproving*) Oh, come off it, man.

(IRIS *tries to unzip Travis's fly. This only unnerves* TRAVIS
more: sexual contact is something he's never really confronted.)

TRAVIS: Listen . . .

IRIS: Don't you want to make it? (*A pause.*) Can't you
make it?

(IRIS *works on* TRAVIS's *crotch off camera. He bats her hand*
away.)

TRAVIS: (*Distraught*) I want to *help* you.
> (TRAVIS *is getting increasingly panicked, but* IRIS *only thinks this is part of his particular thing and tries to overcome it.*)

IRIS: (*Catching on*) You can't make it, can you? (*A pause.*) I can help you.
> (IRIS *lowers her head to go down on* TRAVIS. TRAVIS, *seeing this, jumps up in panic. He stands several feet from* IRIS. *His fly is still open, and the white of his underwear shows through his jeans. He is starting to come apart.*)

TRAVIS: Fuck it! Fuck it! Fuck it! Fuck it! Fuck it! Fuck it! Fuck it!

IRIS: (*Confused*) You can do it in my mouth.

TRAVIS: Don't you understand anything?
> (IRIS *says nothing. After a moment,* TRAVIS *again sits on the bed beside* IRIS. *She no longer tries to make him.*
> *There is a moment of silence.* IRIS *puts her arm around his shoulder.*)

IRIS: You don't *have* to make it, Mister.
> (TRAVIS *rests a moment, collecting himself. Finally, he says:*)

TRAVIS: (*Slowly*) Do you understand why I came here?

IRIS: I think so. I tried to get into your cab one night, and now you want to come and take me away.

TRAVIS: Don't you want to go?

IRIS: I can leave any time I want.

TRAVIS: But that one night?

IRIS: I *was* stoned. That's why they stopped me. When I'm not stoned, I got no place else to go. They just protect me from myself.
> (*There is a pause.* TRAVIS *smiles and shrugs apologetically.*
> TRAVIS *looks at Iris's cigarette. It's burning down to the butt.*)

TRAVIS: Well, I tried.

IRIS: (*Compassionate*) I understand, Mister. It means something, really.

TRAVIS: (*Getting up*) Can I see you again?

IRIS: That's not hard to do.

TRAVIS: No, I mean really. This is nothing for a person to do.

IRIS: Sure. All right. We'll have breakfast. I get up about one o'clock. Tomorrow.

TRAVIS: (*Thinking*) Well tomorrow noon there's a . . . I got
a . . .
(IRIS *is interfering with* TRAVIS's *assassination schedule.*)
IRIS: Well, you want to or not?
TRAVIS: (*Deciding*) OK. It's a date. I'll see you here,
then.
(TRAVIS *turns;* IRIS *smiles.*)
Oh, Iris?
IRIS: Yes?
TRAVIS: My name's Travis.
IRIS: Thank you, Travis.
TRAVIS: So long, Iris. (*A pause.*) Sweet Iris. (*Smiles.*)
(TRAVIS *exits. He closes the door to No. 2 and stands in the
corridor for a moment.
The* OLD MAN *slowly walks from the dark end of the hallway
with Travis's .38 in his hand.* OLD MAN *stands near* TRAVIS,
and checks his watch.)
OLD MAN: (*Holding gun*) I think this is yours, cowboy.
(TRAVIS *reaches in his jacket pocket and pulls out the familiar
crumpled $20 bill. He makes a big show of stuffing the
wrinkled bill into the Old Man's hand. The* OLD MAN *doesn't
understand the significance of it.*)
TRAVIS: (*With restrained anger*) Here's the twenty bucks, old
man. You better damn well spend it right.
(TRAVIS *turns and walks away.*)
OLD MAN: (*As* TRAVIS *walks downstairs*) Come back any time
you want, cowboy. But without the rod – please.
(TRAVIS *does not respond.*)

(*St Regis suite. Noon.*
PALANTINE, TOM *and Palantine's* ASSISTANT *are seated in
garishly decorated suite.*)
ASSISTANT: Well, at least it wasn't chicken.
PALANTINE: It wasn't? I thought it was. It *tasted* like chicken.
TOM: C'mon, Senator. That was a class dinner. The St Regis is
a class joint. That was veal.
PALANTINE: Was it? It sure tasted like chicken to me. (*Pause.*)
Lately, everything tastes like chicken to me.
ASSISTANT: Everything? Got to watch your gut.

PALANTINE: What about it? I took twenty off before we started this thing.

ASSISTANT: And you've put ten of it back on.

PALANTINE: Ten? I don't think so. You really think so? Ten?

TOM: Those TV cameras do. I caught the rally on CBS. You looked a little paunchy.

PALANTINE: I don't think I gained ten pounds.

(PALANTINE *gets up and walks over to the window. Its bars form a cross-sight on his head.*)

PALANTINE: (*Weary, to himself*) Jesus Christ.

(*He looks at the crowded traffic on Fifth Avenue eighteen floors below. It is a mass of yellow.*)

(*Fifth Avenue. Noon.*
Travis's cab pulls away from the yellow mass and heads downtown.)

LATE BREAKFAST

Exterior of downtown coffee shop. Travis's cab is parked near a neighbourhood Bickford's.

TRAVIS *and* IRIS *are having a late breakfast at a middle-class East Side coffee shop. It is about 1.30 p.m.*

IRIS *is dressed more sensibly, wearing jeans and a maroon sweater. Her face is freshly washed and her hair combed out.*

Seen this way, IRIS *looks no different than any other young girl in the big city. Other patrons of the coffee shop most likely assume she is having lunch with her big brother.*

They are both having an all-American breakfast: ham and eggs, large glasses of orange juice, coffee.

Outside her environment, IRIS *seems the more pathetic. She seems unsure, nervous, unable to hold a subject for more than thirty seconds. Her gestures are too broad, her voice too mannered. We sympathize with* TRAVIS'S *paternal response: this girl is in trouble.*

IRIS: . . . and after that Sport and I just started hanging out . . .

TRAVIS: Where is home?

(IRIS *removes her large blue-tinted sunglasses and fishes through her bag for another pair.*)

IRIS: I got so many sunglasses. I couldn't live without my
shades, man. I must have twelve pair of shades.
(*She finds a pink-tinted pair and puts them on.*)

TRAVIS: Where?

IRIS: Pittsburgh.

TRAVIS: I ain't ever been there, but it don't seem like such a
bad place.

IRIS: (*Voice rising*) Why do you want me to go back to my
parents? They hate me. Why do you think I split? There
ain't nothin' there.

TRAVIS: But you can't live like this. It's hell. Girls should live at
home.

IRIS: (*Playfully*) Didn't you ever hear of women's lib?
(*There is a short quick silence;* TRAVIS*'s eyes retract.*)

TRAVIS: (*Ignoring her question*) Young girls are supposed to dress
up, go to school, play with boys, you know, that kinda'
stuff.
(IRIS *places a large gob of jam on her unbuttered toast and
folds the bread over like a hotdog.*)

IRIS: God, are *you* square.

TRAVIS: (*Releasing pent-up tension*) At least I don't walk the

71

streets like a skunk pussy. I don't screw and fuck with killers and junkies.

(IRIS *motions him to lower his voice.*)

IRIS: Who's a killer?

TRAVIS: That fella 'Sport' looks like a killer to me.

IRIS: He never killed nobody. He's a Libra.

TRAVIS: Huh?

IRIS: I'm a Libra too. That's why we get along so well.

TRAVIS: He looks like a killer.

IRIS: I think Cancers make the best lovers. My whole family are air signs.

TRAVIS: He shoots dope too.

IRIS: What makes you so high and mighty? Did you ever look at your own eyeballs in a mirror? You don't get eyes like that from . . .

TRAVIS: He's worse than an animal. Jail's too good for scum like that.

(*There is a brief silence.* IRIS's *mind whirls at 78 rpms. She seems to have three subjects on her mind at a time. She welcomes this opportunity to unburden herself.*)

IRIS: Rock music died in 1970, that's what I think. Before that it was fantastic. I can tell you that. Everybody was crashing, hanging out at the Fillmore. Me and my girlfriend Ann used to go up the fire escape, you know? It was unbelievable. Rock stars everywhere. *The Airplane* – that's my group, man. All Libras. But now everybody's split or got sick or busted. I think I'll move to one of those communes in Vermont, you know? That's where all the smart ones went. I stayed here.

TRAVIS: I never been to a commune. I don't know. I saw pictures in a magazine, and it didn't look very clean to me.

IRIS: Why don't you come to a commune with me?

TRAVIS: Me? I could never go to a place like that.

IRIS: Why not?

TRAVIS: (*Hesitant*) I . . . I don't get along with people like that.

IRIS: You a Scorpian? That's it. You're a Scorpian. I can tell.

TRAVIS: Besides, I've got to stay here.

IRIS: Why?

TRAVIS: I've got something important to do. I can't leave.

IRIS: What's so important?

TRAVIS: I can't say – it's top secret. I'm doing something for the Army. The cab thing is just part-time.

IRIS: You a narc?

TRAVIS: Do I look like a narc?

IRIS: Yeah.

(TRAVIS *breaks out in his big infectious grin, and* IRIS *joins his laughter.*)

IRIS: God, I don't know who's weirder, you or me.

TRAVIS: (*Pause*) What are you going to do about Sport and that old bastard?

IRIS: When?

TRAVIS: When you leave.

IRIS: Just leave 'em. There's plenty of other girls.

TRAVIS: You just gonna leave 'em?

IRIS: (*Astonished*) What should I do? Call the cops?

TRAVIS: Cops don't do nothin'.

IRIS: Sport never treated me bad, honest. Never beat me up once.

TRAVIS: You can't leave 'em to do the same to other girls. You should get rid of them.

IRIS: How?

TRAVIS: (*Shrugs*) I don't know. Just should, though. (*Pause.*) *Somebody* should kill 'em. Nobody'd miss 'em.

IRIS: (*Taken aback*) God. I know where they should have a commune for you. They should have a commune for you at Bellevue.

TRAVIS: (*Apologetic/sheepish*) I'm sorry, Iris. I didn't mean that.

IRIS: You're not much with girls, are you?

TRAVIS: (*Thinks*) Well, Iris, I look at it this way. A lot of girls come into my cab, some of them very beautiful. And I figure all day long men have been after them: trying to touch them, talk to them, ask them out. And they hate it. So I figure the best I can do for them is not to bother them at all. So I don't say a thing. I pretend I'm not even there. I figure they'll understand that and appreciate me for it.

(*It takes* IRIS *a moment to digest this pure example of negative thinking: I am loved to the extent I do not exist.*)

IRIS: Do you really think I should go to the commune?

TRAVIS: I think you should go home, but otherwise I think you

should go. It would be great for you. You have to get away from here. The city's a sewer, you gotta get out of it.
(*Mumbling something about her 'shades' again,* IRIS *fishes through her bag until she comes up with another 99¢ pair of sunglasses and puts them on. She likes these better, she decides.*)

IRIS: Sure you don't want to come with me?

TRAVIS: I can't. Otherwise, I would.

IRIS: I sure hate to go alone.

TRAVIS: I'll give you the money to go. I don't want you to take any from those guys.

IRIS: You don't have to.

TRAVIS: I want to – what else can I do with my money? (*Thinks*) You may not see me again – for a while.

IRIS: What do you mean?
(*Close-up of* TRAVIS.

TRAVIS: My work may take me out of New York.

(*Iris's room. Day.*
SPORT *stands beside the bed.*)

SPORT: What's the matter, baby, don't you feel right?
(IRIS *is wearing her blue-tinted shades.*)

IRIS: It's my stomach. I got the flu.
(SPORT *puts his hands on her hips. He is slowly, carefully, smoothly manipulating her. It's the stoned black hustle.*)

SPORT: Oh, baby, there ain't no flu. You know that, baby.

IRIS: Honest, Sport.
(SPORT *puts some slow soul music on the stereo.*)

SPORT: You're just tired, baby. You just need your man. I am your man, you know. You are my woman. I wouldn't be nothing without you.
(SPORT *slowly grinds his hips to hers.* IRIS *starts to move with him. This is what she really wanted. Her man's attention.*)
I know this may not mean anything to you, baby, but sometimes I get so emotional, sometimes I think, I wish every man could have what I have now, that every woman could be loved the way I love you. I wish every man could be as happy with his woman as I am with you now. I go home and I think what it would be without you, and then I thank God for you. I think to myself, man, you are so

74

lucky. You got a woman who loves you, who needs you, a woman who keeps you strong. It's just you and me. I'm nothing without you. I can go like this for ever and ever. We can do it, baby. You and me. Just you and me.
(SPORT *slowly rubs his crotch into her.* IRIS *smiles. She is happy. The music rises.*)

GOD'S LONELY MAN

Firing Range. Day. TRAVIS *stands at the firing range blasting the .44 Magnum with a rapid-fire vengeance.*
He puts down one gun, picks up the next, then the next. Quickly reloading, he fires again.
The targets spin and dance under his barrage. The piercing sound of gunshots rings through the air.)

(*Inside Travis's apartment.*
TRAVIS *is again writing at the table. His western shirt is open, exposing his bare chest.*
A note of despair and doom has entered into TRAVIS's *normally monotone narration voice: this will be the last entry in his diary.*
TRAVIS: (*Voice over*) My whole life has pointed in one direction. I see that now. There never has been any choice for me.
(*Lengthy point-of-view shot from Travis's taxi: we see New York's nightlife as* TRAVIS *sees it. Camera tracks down midtown sidewalks in slightly slow motion. There we see couples, walking in slowing motion: young couples, middle-aged couples, hookers and johns, girlfriends, boyfriends, business friends – the whole world matched up in pairs, and* TRAVIS *left wandering alone in the night.*
Others would notice the breasts, the asses, the faces, but not TRAVIS: *he notices the girl's hand that rubs the hair on her boyfriend's neck, the hand that hangs lightly on his shoulder, the nuzzling kiss in the ear.*)
Loneliness has followed me all my life. The life of loneliness pursues, me wherever I go: in bars, cars, coffee shops, theatres, stores, sidewalks. There is no escape. I am God's lonely man.
(TRAVIS's *point-of-view: another neighbourhood, later in the*

night. Still in slightly slow motion. The crowds are more sparse here, the streets darker, a junkie shudders in a doorway, a wino pukes into a trash can, a street-walker meets a prospective client.)

I am not a fool. I will no longer fool myself. I will no longer let myself fall apart, become a joke and object of ridicule. I know there is no longer any hope. I cannot continue this hollow, empty fight. I must sleep. What hope is there for me?

(Inside Travis's apartment.

TRAVIS, *his shirt fastened, stands beside table.*

Close-up: he lays a brief hand-written letter on the table. We read it.

> Dear Iris,
>   This money should be enough for your trip. By the time you read this I will be dead.
>
>   Travis

TRAVIS *stacks five crisp hundred-dollar bills beside the letter, folds them up with the letter, and puts them into an envelope.)*

(A short while later. TRAVIS has cleaned up his apartment. Everything is neat and orderly.

Camera pans across room: the mattress is bare and flattened out, the floor is spotless, the cans and bottles of food and pills put out of sight. The wall is still covered with Palantine political paraphernalia, but when we reach the desk we see only four items there: an open diary and three loaded revolvers: .44, .38, .25.

TRAVIS, *freshly shaved and neatly dressed, stands in the middle of his clean room. The empty holster hangs on his shoulder. Metal .25 gliders can be seen under the slit in his right sleeve. He turns towards table.*

TRAVIS, *envelope in hand, closes the door behind him and walks down the corridor.*

He passes an open door and we are surprised to see the room is empty – and trashed. TRAVIS *lives in a decaying, if not condemned, building.*

Outside, TRAVIS *places the envelope to* IRIS *in his mail box.)*

(*Back in apartment, camera closes on revolvers lying on the table in neat array.*)

THERE IS AN ASSASSIN

Sound of a political rally: cheering, laughing, a band playing, talking.
Afternoon. A crowd of about 500 is assembled before a platform outside a Brooklyn union hall. A Dixieland band is playing on the platform.
Close-up of CHARLES PALANTINE's *feet climbing out of a limousine. There is a roar from the crowd near by.*
PALANTINE, *a bulky* SECRET SERVICE MAN *to the right and left of him, pushes his way through the crowd toward the platform. Still cameras click, and TV cameras purr.*
Slight timecut: PALANTINE *is speaking on the platform.*
Travis's empty taxi sits parked a few blocks away from rally. At this distance, the rally sounds are almost indistinguishable.
Close-up of Travis's boots walking. They make their way past one person, then two, then a cluster of three or four. Sounds of rally increase.

We see a full-figure shot of TRAVIS: *he is standing alone in an opening near the fringes of the crowd.*

TRAVIS *looks like the most suspicious human being alive. His hair is cropped short, he wears mirror-reflecting glasses. His face is pallid and drained of colour, his lips are pursed and drawn tight. He looks from side to side. One can now see the full effect of* TRAVIS's *lack of sleep and insufficient diet – he looks sick and frail.*

Even though it is a warm June day, TRAVIS *is bundled up in a shirt, sweater and Army jacket buttoned from top to bottom. Under his jacket are several large lumps, causing his upper torso to look larger than it should. He is slightly hunched over and his hands shoved into his pockets.*

Anyone scanning the crowd would immediately light upon TRAVIS *and think, 'There is an asssassin.'*

TRAVIS *pulls the vial of red pills from his pocket and swallows a couple.*

The SECRET SERVICE MAN *is standing beside the platform, scanning the crowd. It is the same* SECRET SERVICE MAN TRAVIS *spoke to at the first rally.* TOM, *dressed in a conservative suit, stands beside him.*

PALANTINE *is wrapping up his short speech.*

PALANTINE: . . . and with your help we will go on to victory at the polls Tuesday – (*Applause.*)

(TRAVIS *begins moving up into the crowd*)

– on to victory in Miami Beach next month.

(*Applause mounts*)

– and on to victory next November!

PALANTINE *steps back, smiling and receiving the applause. Then, nodding at the* SECRET SERVICE MAN, *he descends the stairs and prepares to work his way through the crowd.*

TRAVIS *unbuttons the middle two buttons of his jacket, opening access to his holster. With the other hand he checks the .44 hooked behind his back.*

PALANTINE *smiles and shakes a few of the many hands outstretched towards him.*

The SECRET SERVICE MAN, *scanning the crowd, spots something that interests him. He looks closely.*

SECRET SERVICE MAN's *point of view:* TRAVIS, *his face intense, pushes his way through the crowd.*

PALANTINE *works his way through the crowd and cameras.*

78

SECRET SERVICE MAN *motions to* SECOND SECRET SERVICE
MAN *and points in* TRAVIS'*s direction.*
TRAVIS *slips his hand into his jacket.*
The SECOND SECRET SERVICE MAN *converges on* TRAVIS
from the side.
TRAVIS *and* PALANTINE *draw closer to each other.*
SECRET SERVICE MAN, *walking just behind* PALANTINE,
grabs the candidate's hand and pulls him backwards.
PALANTINE *looks sharply back at* SECRET SERVICE MAN *who
motions for him to take a slightly altered route.*
TRAVIS *sees this: his eyes meet the* SECRET SERVICE MAN'*s.
He recognizes the situation. To his right he spots the* SECOND
SECRET SERVICE MAN.
TRAVIS'*s eyes meet* PALANTINE'*s: candidate and would-be
assassin exchange quick glances.*
TRAVIS *hastily works his way back through the crowd. He
hears the* SECRET SERVICE MAN'*s voice call out.*)
SECRET SERVICE MAN: Detain that man!
(*Overhead shot reveals* TRAVIS *has the jump on his pursuers.
He is breaking free of the crowd while they are still mired in it.*
TRAVIS, *free of his pursuers, quickly makes his way down the
sidewalks. The* SECRET SERVICE MEN *look futilely about.*
TRAVIS *jumps in his cab. Sweat covers his face.*)

TOWARDS THE KILL

*The film is moving fast now; it pushes hard and straight towards its
conclusion. We're moving towards the kill.*
*Late afternoon. Travis's taxi skids around a corner and speeds into
Manhattan.*
TRAVIS *checks his mail slot: the letter to* IRIS *has already been
picked up by the mailman.*
Stripped to the waist, TRAVIS *walks back and forth across his
apartment wiping his torso with a bath towel.*
*He begins dressing: he straps the Army combat knife to his calf; he
reflexes the metal gliders and the Colt .25 on his right forearm.*

SPORT *stands in his doorway on the Lower East Side. It is early
evening. A pudgy middle-aged white* PRIVATE COP *walks up to*
SPORT. *The two men laugh, slap each other on the back and*

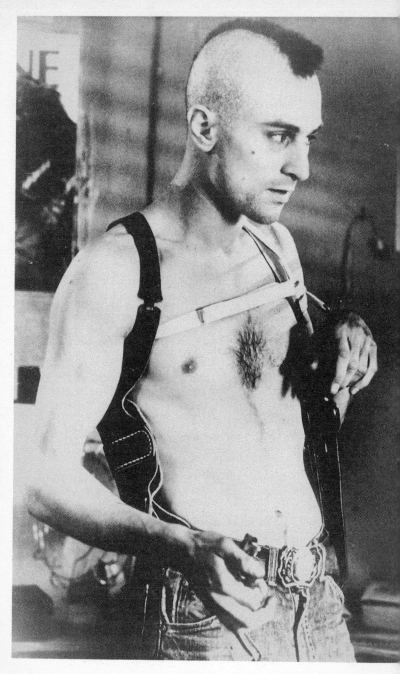

exchange a soul shake. They discuss a little private business and the private cop walks off in the direction of Iris's apartment.

TRAVIS *straps on holster and fits the .38 Special into it.*

PRIVATE COP *walks down block.*

TRAVIS *hooks the huge Magnum into the back of his belt. He puts on his Army jacket and walks out through the door.*

PRIVATE COP *turns up darkened stairway to Iris's apartment.*

Night has fallen. Travis's taxi careens down 10th Avenue. He speeds, honks, accelerates quickly. The glare of speeding yellow and red lights flash through the night.

TRAVIS's *point of view: A pedestrian attempts to flag down the taxi, but quickly steps back up on the kerb when he sees* TRAVIS *has no intention of stopping for anything.*

SPORT *maintains his post in the dark doorway. He waves to a girl who passes, and she waves back.*

Travis's taxi screeches to a stop and parks obliquely against the kerb.

THE SLAUGHTER

TRAVIS *walks down the block to the doorway where* SPORT *stands. Camera tracks with* TRAVIS.
Without slowing down, TRAVIS *walks up to* SPORT *and puts his arm on his shoulder in a gesture of friendliness.*
TRAVIS: Hey, Sport. How are things?
SPORT: (*Shrugs*) OK, cowboy.
TRAVIS: (*Needling him*) How are things in the *pimp* business, hey Sport?
SPORT: What's going on?
TRAVIS: I'm here to see Iris.
SPORT: Iris?
    (TRAVIS *pushes* SPORT *back into the dark recesses of the corridor.*)
    Wha – ?
TRAVIS: Yeah, Iris. You know anybody by that name?
SPORT: No. (*A pause.*) Hillbilly, you'd better get your wise ass outa here and quick, or you're gonna be in trouble.

(TRAVIS *is being propelled by an inner force, a force which takes him past the boundaries of reason and self-control.*)

TRAVIS: (*With restrained anger*) You carry a gun?

(SPORT *looks into* TRAVIS*'s eyes, saying nothing: he realizes the seriousness of the situation.*

TRAVIS *pulls his .38 Special and holds it on* SPORT*, pushing him even further back against the wall.*)

Get it.

SPORT (*Submissive*) Hey, Mister, I don't know what's going on here. This don't make any sense.

TRAVIS: (*Demanding*) Show it to me.

(SPORT *reluctantly pulls a .32 calibre pistol (a 'purse gun') from his pocket and holds it limply.*

TRAVIS *sticks his .38 into* SPORT*'s gut and discharges it. There is a muffled blast, followed by a muted scream of pain.*)

Now suck on that.

(*Agony and shock cross* SPORT*'s face as he slumps to the floor.*

TRAVIS *turns and walks away before* SPORT *even hits.*

As TRAVIS *walks away,* SPORT *can be seen struggling in the background.*

TRAVIS*, his gun slipped into his jacket, walks quickly up the sidewalk.*

Around the corner, TRAVIS *walks into the darkened stairway leading to Iris's apartment.*

As he walks up the stairs, he pulls the .44 Magnum from behind his back and transfers the .38 Special to his left hand. He walks up the steps, a pistol dangling from each hand.

At the top of the stairs, TRAVIS *spots the* OLD MAN *sitting at the far end of the dark corridor. The* OLD MAN *starts to get up when* TRAVIS *discharges the mighty .44 at him. BLAAM! The hallway reverberates with shock waves and gun powder.*

The OLD MAN *staggers at the end of the corridor: his right hand has been blown off at the forearm.*

There is the sharp sound of a gunshot behind TRAVIS*: his face grimaces in pain. A bullet has ripped through the left side of his neck. Blood flows over his left shoulder.*

Travis's .44 flies into the air.

TRAVIS *looks down the stairway: there* SPORT *lies choking in a puddle of his own blood. He has struggled far enough to fire one shot.*)

Falling, TRAVIS *drills another .38 slug into* SPORT's *back but* SPORT *is already dead.*

TRAVIS *slumps to his knees. Down the corridor the* OLD MAN *with a bloody stump is struggling towards him.* TRAVIS *turns his .38 towards the* OLD MAN.

The door to No. 2 opens: IRIS's *scream is heard in the background. The bulky frame of the* PRIVATE COP *fills the doorway. His blue shirt is open, in his hand hangs a .38 service revolver.*

The PRIVATE COP *raises his gun and shoots* TRAVIS. TRAVIS, *blood gushing from his right shoulder, sinks to the floor. His .38 clangs down the stairs.*

The OLD MAN *grows closer.* TRAVIS *smashes his right arm against the wall, miraculously, the small Colt .25 glides down his forearm into his palm.*

TRAVIS *fills the* PRIVATE COP's *face full of bullet holes.*

The PRIVATE COP, *screaming, crashes back into the room.*

The OLD MAN *crashes atop* TRAVIS. *The .25 falls from* TRAVIS's *hand.*

Both men are bleeding profusely as they thrash into Iris's room. IRIS *hides behind the old red velvet sofa, her face frozen in fright.*

84

TRAVIS, *trapped under the heavy* OLD MAN, *reaches down with his right hand and pulls the combat knife from his right calf. Just as* TRAVIS *draws back the knife, the* OLD MAN *brings his huge left palm crashing down on* TRAVIS: *the* OLD MAN's *palm is impaled on the knife.*

The OLD MAN *screams in pain.*

Police sirens are heard in the background.

With a great effort, TRAVIS *turns over, pinning the* OLD MAN *to the floor. The bloody knife blade sticks through his upturned hand.*

TRAVIS *reaches over with his right hand and picks up the revolver of the now dead private cop.*

TRAVIS *hoists himself up and sticks the revolver into the* OLD MAN's *mouth.*

The OLD MAN's *voice is full of pain and ghastly fright:*)

OLD MAN: Don't kill me! Don't kill me!

(IRIS *screams in background.* TRAVIS *looks up.*)

IRIS: Don't kill him, Travis! Don't kill him!

(TRAVIS *fires the revolver, blowing the back of the* OLD MAN's *head off and silencing his protests.*

The police sirens screech to a halt. Sound of police officers running up the stairs.

TRAVIS *struggles up and collapses on the red velvet sofa, his blood-soaked body blending with the velvet.*

IRIS *retreats in fright against the far wall.*

First uniformed police officer rushes into room, drawn gun in hand. Other policemen can be heard running up the stairs.

TRAVIS *looks helplessly up at the officer. He forms his bloody hand into a pistol, raises it to his forehead and, his voice croaking in pain, makes the sound of a pistol discharging.*

TRAVIS: Pgghew! Pgghew!

(*Out-of-breath fellow officers join the first policeman. They survey the room.*

TRAVIS's *head slumps against the sofa.*

IRIS *is huddled in the corner, shaking.*

Live sound ceases. Overhead slow-motion tracking shot surveys the damage: from IRIS *shaking against the blood-spattered wall; to* TRAVIS's *blood-soaked body lying on the sofa; to the* OLD MAN *with half a head, a bloody stump for one hand and a knife sticking out of the other; to police officers staring in* amazement; to the PRIVATE COP's bullet-ridden face trapped near the doorway; to puddles of blood and a lonely .44 Magnum lying on the hallway carpet; down the blood-speckled stairs on which lies a nickle-plated .38 Smith and Wesson Special; to the foot of the stairs where SPORT's body is hunched over a pool of blood and a small .32 lies near his hand; to crowds huddled around the doorway, held back by police officers; past red flashing lights, running policemen and parked police cars; to the ongoing nightlife of the Lower East Side, curious but basically unconcerned, looking then heading its own way.)*

LETTER FROM PITTSBURGH

Outside Travis's apartment. Day. It is early autumn. The trees are losing their leaves.
Slow tracking shot across inside of apartment. Room appears pretty much the same, although there is a new portable TV and an inexpensive easy chair.

[Visual]	[Audio]
Track begins at table and works across room to the mattress. We see these items: On the table rests the diary, closed. A desk calendar stands on the table: it is October. Across the wall, where the Palantine clippings once hung, there are now a series of new newspaper clippings. They read from right to left. The first is a full back page from the New York Daily News. Headline reads: 'CABBIE BATTLES GANGSTER'S. There	Throughout the track, we hear the voice of a middle-aged uneducated man reading in voice over. It is the voice of IRIS'S FATHER, reading a letter he sent to TRAVIS, and which TRAVIS has tacked to his wall. IRIS'S FATHER: (Voice over) 'Dear Mr Bickle, I can't say how happy Mrs Steensma and I were to hear that you are well and recuperating. We tried to visit you at the hospital when we were in New York to pick up

*Screenwriter's note: The screenplay has been moving at a reasonably realistic level until this prolonged slaughter. The slaughter itself is a gory extension of violence, more surreal than real.
    The slaughter is the moment Travis has been heading for all his life, and where this screenplay has been heading for over 85 pages. It is the release of all that cumulative pressure; it is a reality unto itself. It is the psychopath's Second Coming.

are large photos of police
standing in Iris's room after the
slaughter, and a picture of
TRAVIS*'s cabbie mug shot.*
Underneath this there is a more
discreet clipping, without a
photo, from the New York
Times. *Two-column headline*
reads: 'CABBIE SHOOT-OUT,
THREE DEAD'.
A follow-up story from the
News*: two-column photo shows*
a plain middle-aged couple
sitting in a middle-class living
room. Two-column headline
reads: 'PARENTS EXPRESS
SHOCK, GRATITUDE'.
A two-column Daily News *story*
without photo. Headline reads:
'TAXI-DRIVER HERO TO
RECOVER'.
A one-column two-paragraph
News *story stuck on an obscure*
page. Headline reads: 'CABBIE
RETURNS TO JOB'.
At the end of the clippings, a
letter is tacked to the wall. It is
a simple letter, handwritten on
plain white paper. The
handwriting belongs to someone
who has made a conscious effort
to appear neat and orderly. We
recognize from some of the words
that it is the same letter that is
being read in voice over.
When we finally arrive at the
mattress, we find it is barren. A
pillow and blanket (new
purchases) are folded at the head
of the bed.

Iris, but you were still in a
coma.

There is no way we can
repay you for returning our
Iris to us. We thought we had
lost her, but now our lives are
full again. Needless to say,
you are something of a hero
around this household.

I'm sure you want to know
about Iris. She is back in
school and working hard. The
transition has been very hard
for her, as you can well
imagine, but we have taken
steps to see she never has
cause to run away again.

In conclusion, Mrs
Steensma and I would like to
again thank you from the
bottom of our hearts.
Unfortunately, we cannot
afford to come to New York
again to thank you in person,
or we surely would. But if you
should ever come to
Pittsburgh, you would find
yourself a most welcome guest
in our home.

Our deepest thanks,

Burt and Ivy Steensma'

Outside the Plaza Hotel. Night.
Four cabs stand in the waiting line in front of the hotel.
Near the entrance, TRAVIS *and* WIZARD *stand in the light, talking.*
TRAVIS's *hair is almost fully grown back to its normal length.*
TRAVIS *wears the same clothes – cowboy boots, jeans, western shirt,*
Army jacket – but he isn't wearing a gun. There is a thick scar on
the left side of his neck.
WIZARD *is speaking.*

WIZARD: A private owner wanted to swap wheels. Now my
tyres were brand new. 'Give me a couple days,' I says.
(CHARLIE T *parks his cab in line and walks towards* TRAVIS
and WIZARD.)

CHARLIE T: Howdy, Wizard, Killer.
(CHARLIE T *points his pistol/finger at* TRAVIS, *fires, says*
'*Pow*' *and laughs.*)
(*Casual joking.*) Don't mess with the Killer.

TRAVIS: (*Smiles*) Hey Charlie T.

WIZARD: Howsit, Charlie? (*A pause.*) Hey, Travis, I think you
gotta fare.
(*They all turn. Point-of-view shot of doorman closing rear door*
of Travis's taxi.)

TRAVIS: Shit.
(*He runs off.*)

CHARLIE T: Take it slow, Killer.
(TRAVIS *waves back to* CHARLIE T *and* WIZARD *as he runs*
around cab and jumps in the driver's seat.)
(*Travis's taxi pulls away.*
Close-up of TRAVIS *at the wheel. From the back, a* FEMALE
VOICE *says:*)

FEMALE VOICE: 34 East 56th Street.
(TRAVIS *recognizes the voice. He looks in the rear-view mirror:*
it is BETSY.
TRAVIS *says nothing: he heads towards 56th Street. After a*
silence, BETSY *speaks.*)

BETSY: Hello, Travis.

TRAVIS: Hello, Betsy.
(*There is an uneasy pause.*)
I see where Palantine got the nomination.

BETSY: Yes. It won't be long now. Seventeen days.

TRAVIS: Well, I hope he wins.

    (*There is another pause.*)

BETSY: (*Concerned*) How are *you*, Travis? I read about you in the papers.

TRAVIS: Oh, I got over that. It was nothing, really. The papers always blow these things up. (*A pause.*) A little stiffness. That'll go away. I just sleep more, that's all.

    (*Travis's taxi pulls up at 34 East 56th Street.*)

    Here we are.

    (BETSY *digs in her purse.*)

    (*Protesting*) No, no please. This fare's on me. Please.

BETSY: Thank you, Travis.

    (BETSY *gets out of the cab and stands by the right front window, which is open.*

    TRAVIS *prepares to drive away.*

    Travis?

TRAVIS: Yeah?

BETSY: Maybe I'll see you again sometime, huh?

TRAVIS: (*With a thin smile*) Sure.

    (BETSY *steps away from the kerb and* TRAVIS *drives off. She watches his taxi.*

    Camera follows Travis's taxi as it slowly disappears down 56th Street.)

THE END

SELECT SOUNDTRACKS

CDs available for Faber and Faber titles

NATIONAL FILM THEATRE

The NFT is the world's greatest cinema, with the world's biggest and best choice of films.

From cult classics and the latest Hollywood hits to world cinema and silent masterpieces; over 2000 films to enjoy every year.

Membership costs £11.95 (£8 concessions) and gives all these benefits;

£1 off every ticket (for you and up to 3 guests)

Monthly programme mailings

Priority booking for all screenings, including the London Film Festival

£30 worth of Connoisseur Video vouchers

Exclusive book and video offers.

Join the NFT now and we'll send you a voucher for £4.75 to see one great film for free.*

JOIN THE NFT
THE ALL YEAR ROUND FILM FESTIVAL

TO JOIN THE NFT, SIMPLY RING 0171 815 1374 OR WRITE TO
MEMBERSHIP DEPARTMENT, NFT, FREEPOST SE8 223, LONDON SE1 8YY

(*Offer applies to new membership application only, cannot be used in conjuction with any other offer or discount and is subject to availability.)